KATE McCALLUM
& JULIA NEWBOULD

THE
JOY
OF
MONEY

are media books
Published in 2020 by Are Media Books, Australia. Reprinted 2021. Are Media Books is a division of Are Media Pty Ltd.

Authors Kate McCallum & Julia Newbould

ARE MEDIA
Chief executive officer Brendon Hill

ARE MEDIA BOOKS
General manager: publishing Sally Eagle
Creative director Hannah Blackmore
Designer Kelsie Walker
Operations manager David Scotto

Printed in China
by 1010 Printing International
A catalogue record for this book is available
from the National Library of Australia.
ISBN 978-1-92586-569-1

Published by Are Media Books,
a division of Are Media Pty Ltd,
54 Park St, Sydney; GPO Box 4088,
Sydney, NSW 2001, Australia
Ph +61 2 8116 9334
www.aremedia.com.au

ORDER BOOKS
phone 1300 322 007 (within Australia)
or order online at *www.aremediabooks.com.au*

DISCLAIMER

This book is general in nature and provides information in summary form only. It should not be considered a comprehensive statement on any matter and you should not rely on it as such. It is also not intended to take the place of professional advice. It does not take into account your personal objectives, financial situation or needs and so you need to consider (with or without the assistance of an adviser) whether this information is appropriate to your needs, objectives and circumstances before acting on it. This book does not recommend any particular products or services. Any projections provided are purely estimates, they are not guaranteed, and may vary with changing circumstances. This information is provided for persons in Australia only and is not provided for the use of any person who is in any other country.

KATE McCALLUM & JULIA NEWBOULD

THE
JOY
OF
MONEY

THE *Australian woman's*
GUIDE TO FINANCIAL INDEPENDENCE

CONTENTS

Like many women, I have had a complicated relationship with my finances.

I grew up on our family cherry and apple orchard that had been devastated by the Black Sunday bushfires 18 months before I was born. The business did not become profitable again for almost 20 years. My parents were careful with money and my early years were defined by the need to be frugal.

JULIE BISHOP

Throughout my teenage years and at university I had a myriad of part time jobs. Thereafter, I was fortunate in my professional careers and achieved financial independence as a young adult. However, this led to a level of complacency and a lack of attention to my savings and investments at crucial times.

Many of my financial decisions were not at the recommendation of a qualified adviser and were often following suggestions from friends, some who had great intentions but little relevant experience. Secondly, proper budgeting was an afterthought, meaning my finances were out of balance at times.

With experience comes wisdom and some of the lessons I learned are in this book, *The Joy of Money: The Australian woman's guide to financial independence.*

As Kate and Julia point out, it is important for everyone to pay close attention to their financial situation however it is more vital for women.

The Australian Human Rights Commission reports that women currently aged 45-59 have on average far less funds in superannuation than men of a comparable age, with the current average payout from superannuation for women 33% less than for men[1].

The pay-gap still exists with female full-time workers typically paid 16% less than their male counterparts, while performing the same role.

The Global Gender Gap Report 2018 by the World Economic Forum provides assessments of 149 nations against a 2006 baseline.

One of the interesting findings is that while the global gender gap in education has declined to 4.4%, women still held only 34% of managerial positions in their careers. This has been a feature in Australia for many years, where women are increasingly likely to graduate from university and yet continue to struggle for promotion to senior or executive levels.

It is reported that women spend more than double the hours each week in unpaid work of caring for family and other domestic chores than their male counterparts. Women also spend more time out of the workforce caring for family.

A fascinating but deeply troubling finding of the report is that if current trends are maintained, gender gaps will be eliminated in Western Europe in around 61 years, 70 years in Asia, 74 years in South and Central America, 153 years in the Middle East, 171 years in the Pacific and 165 years in North America. These figures illustrate why women must focus more fully on their finances and to strive for financial independence.

Women must better understand the options and possibilities available to them.

Knowledge is power. In this context, knowledge starts with learning to be financially literate, by seeking out guidance from others with more relevant experience, including obtaining the advice of professionals with expertise in budgeting and investing.

Self-help books can be a great starting point for any woman who is seeking the path to better personal financial management. We should all read this book, wherever we may be on that path.

- Julie Bishop, former MP and Deputy Leader of the Liberal Party

1 https://www.humanrights.gov.au/our-work/gender-gap-retirement-savings

LET'S START AT THE VERY BEGINNING

SMART, SAVVY & FINANCIALLY FIT FOR OUR FUTURE

Women need a room of their own, as Virginia Woolf so rightly wrote. Women also need to have money of their own – it gives us freedom, choices and possibilities. With this in mind, we wanted to focus our women friends' attention on money – so we wrote this book.

There is no one size that fits all. There are common issues and matters we should all be thinking about, or should know. We may not answer all your questions but we can provide insights and steer you in the right direction.

If we can help you and your friends start on this journey to freedom we will feel that we've done our job well. If we can help you get there quicker, we'll be very happy and if you are able to share what you've learned from us then we'll feel joyful.

Money and finances may be seen by many women as more a man's domain – which is probably not surprising given that much of the language of money is masculine (build wealth, trade stocks, construct a portfolio). And some women told us that while they feel smart in their own space, they don't feel smart about money.

Women told us that other things in life took priority ahead of money. The daily juggle of relationships, kids, parents, friends, career, education and health simply didn't leave the time needed to keep up with money and financial matters.

Women also told us that they didn't know where to start with money, and without step one, they couldn't move further.

"The Joy of Money: The Australian woman's guide to financial independence" is designed to address these barriers.

There is a lot of jargon associated with the world of money and finance. We don't believe in jargon. We believe that it has been used in finance circles to exclude people, and while the terms may be complex the concepts are not. We have removed unnecessary jargon from our book and explained key concepts in practical ways.

To save you time, we've included "quick step" guides in each chapter. If you don't have the head space to work through the whole chapter, these points should get you started on the small steps that can make a big difference.

We've also designed the chapters so that you can work through them in order – building your personal plan as you go. You can also jump in and out, going directly to the chapters where you most require guidance. Either way, you will find valuable insights and practical steps to help you to make good decisions and move forward.

This book can't give you specific investment recommendations nor will it give you a one-size fits all

YOU NEED MONEY TO BE FINANCIALLY INDEPENDENT, AND YOU NEED FINANCIAL INDEPENDENCE TO HAVE CHOICES ABOUT YOUR LIFE AND YOUR GOALS.

strategy but it can give you new ideas and a greater understanding of money and finance so that you can take action.

It should also give you the confidence to seek professional advice and understand some of the terminology and concepts that a financial adviser, accountant or lawyer may use.

There will always be distractions coming between you and your future finances – your job may be taking all your free time, your children may be taking the rest and you may feel you haven't the head space for it (hopefully, since you've bought this book that isn't the case).

We've included a range of profiles of other women, that you might feel are in similar straits to you, to give you an idea of how others are planning on reaching their goals. These can give you ideas of how other people are thinking and provide a few tips on matters you may not have considered.

While we've included a note on whether or not they've sought financial advice, we would recommend advice for most people – to help with strategies you might not have considered, to act as a coach and a conscience on your journey and to give you greater peace of mind.

Please remember it's not too late – it's never too late. One of the biggest mistakes, we believe, is to do nothing.

Whatever you do, continue to take an interest in your finances. You need money to be financially independent, and you need financial independence to have choices in your life and for your goals.

There's no need to feel guilty about the past – it's the past. Whether we've got all the super we should have had, or whether we've sacrificed savings for shoes, or if we lost money in bad investments, or a bad relationships, let's agree we start here today. We are where we are and regrets will not help. They may be lessons you can tell someone younger but that's it. Let's agree to look ahead and see what we can do right now.

> **PLEASE REMEMBER IT'S NOT TOO LATE – IT'S NEVER TOO LATE. ONE OF THE BIGGEST MISTAKES, WE BELIEVE, IS TO DO NOTHING.**

ABOUT THE AUTHORS

I started this book when I was at a crossroads in my job. I wanted a change but didn't know if I could afford it.

What was holding me back? Confidence about my finances. What do I really need to live on? What are my options for that money? Retraining, working part time, a new job? If I stayed – how could I manage money better so I could make sure I'm better set up financially next time I crave a change.

This book is to help you reach your goals – and be confident when times get tough that you're on your way.

I've been working with financial advisers for nearly 20 years and, while I'm not an adviser, I have learned a lot along the way.

I bought my first property aged 24. I put my entire cadet journalist wage into repayments, I worked in a restaurant to pay for incidentals, I tutored and I took no notice of the bank's minimum repayments, choosing to put all I could afford into the loan on a weekly basis. Within the first 18 months I was paying the interest and making inroads into the loan principal. After a few years I was able to rent it out

JULIA NEWBOULD
FINANCIAL WRITER & EDITOR

and live overseas. On my return I bought my current home and have been in a holding pattern ever since.

My standard of living is good but not my savings. Now that I realise I need money to fund my next chapter, I have some regrets. I, too, need to act on the tips in our book!

KATE McCALLUM
FINANCIAL ADVISER

I confess, I haven't always been smart about money. As a teen, I was pretty savvy. I entered art and writing competitions offering prize money and I earned a healthy income. This was good as I loved music and fashion. I couldn't afford designer clothes but I was fortunate that my grandmother was a stunning seamstress. And so my cash would go on designer patterns and beautiful fabrics which she helped me transform into fabulous fashion. I was also fortunate that my grandmother was savvy about money. I remember her telling me that I needed to look after myself financially. Wise words. I forgot her wisdom when I fell in love. In the words of songstress Taylor Swift: I am smart unless I am really, really in love, and then I am ridiculously stupid. I stepped aside from managing my money – and things unravelled. Luckily, I was in my 20s and still young, and fortunate to have a good education, career and lots of drive.

Like Julia, I live a good life. I save and I spend – but consciously, on the things that really matter to me and give me joy. So, my words of wisdom are: take charge of your money and your life. Make conscious choices on what you save and spend as this is the heart of being smart about money.

Take charge of your money and your life.

AGES AND STAGES

Starting out

• Financially organised – focus on the "pay yourself first" principle. This is where you set a target amount of savings and treat it like mortgage/rent – that is rather than saving what's left after spending, you spend what's left after saving. (And of course, you keep doing this throughout life.)

• Create a Will and Power of Attorney. Regardless of whether you have assets, this is really to ensure you don't leave a mess for your loved ones to clean up.

• Check your super investment option. If you're in your 20s or 30s, you're unlikely to need your super for 30+ years – so you can have a high proportion in growth assets (if the value goes down with market movements it shouldn't impact you because you're not using this money yet).

• Check your super death benefit nominations.

• Saving – create a buffer of six months' worth of expenses.

• Investing – get started. Top up super (even when starting out, we suggest that you may target 12%). For personal investments, look for low cost investment options.

• If you want to save for a first home, find out about the First Home Saver Super Scheme (which is a very tax-effective way to save for a first home through super).

• Always always always repay credit cards each month. Do not use personal loans for anything (including car finance) – they have interest rates in the double digits.

Building your Career

• Negotiate pay, build your skills and manage career. This is all about maximising your human capital.

• Automatically invest most of your bonus – you could do something like 35% to super; 35% to investment; 30% to spend.

• Automatically increase savings with any pay rises.

• Re-check insurances when your salary increases to ensure you have enough.

• If you marry or partner, renew your Wills and Estate Planning including super beneficiary nominations. Remember marriage voids an existing Will.

Career break / kids

• Plan for a career break by living on one salary for 12 months before you take your break. Not only will it help you plan for less income, it will also help you build a buffer for increased expenses.

• Keep up contributions to super – spouse contributions, personal contributions, maybe even using super splitting during a career break.

• Re-check insurances – dependents mean you need to think about life insurance.

• Think about Child Trauma insurance for children aged 2+.

• If you have a mortgage, keep up repayments before starting personal investments.

50s

• Boost your super.

• Re-check insurances – you may not need as much if kids are becoming independent.

• Direct any cost savings (e.g. school fees, mortgage) to other investments (super, mortgage, investment).

• Ensure adult children have, at least, income protection.

• If you divorce or re-partner, re-do your Will and Estate Planning including super beneficiary nominations.

5 OF THE BIGGEST MONEY MISTAKES PEOPLE MAKE

1. Doing nothing. It's so easy for time to slip by. Start now.

2. Assuming that earning a good income will do the trick. A good income won't guarantee that you'll be financially fit. And a good income today is not a guaranteed in the future. As Maria said: "Most of us spend a lot of time earning money and very little time planning it."

3. Not using tax concessions. The main one is super.

4. Not being conscious about cashflow. Sally said: "If I'd known how to take care of my cashflow in my 20s, I would have spent the next couple of decades living less out of fear". Cashflow is king.

5. Not staying engaged with your money. Kathryn said in her marriage she had no idea how much the mortgage was. "It wasn't that my husband took my power – I was not engaged. Today I have re-connected with my money, I count every dollar and I'm in control".

1

VALUES, GOALS
& PRIORITIES

YOU NEED TO KNOW YOUR DESTINATION BEFORE YOU START THE JOURNEY. THINK OF YOUR FINANCES AS JUST THE MEANS TO TAKE YOU WHERE YOU WANT TO GO

KNOWING ME, KNOWING YOU

It's more difficult to reach a destination if you don't know where you want to go. And then it's harder to get there if you're not sure of the travel arrangements.

We all have different destinations in mind. We also have different modes of transport, duration and style that we're comfortable with in getting there.

To start your journey to independence and freedom you need to plan your means and method very clearly.

You need to have your values, goals and priorities in clear sight. They don't need to be too specific – you don't have to know where you want to travel and when, or what renovations you plan in the future, or the car you will buy next, but you do have to have basic ideas such as when you'd like to stop working, what you'd like to do in the next couple of years and other big things that you will need in the future – education expenses, a home upgrade, a boat or the trip to Antarctica that you've always dreamed of.

If you want to be happy with how you manage and spend your money, the secret is to spend in line with your values. Values are core to who you are – they don't really change very much over time.

So, the first step when you're preparing a money plan is to identify your values.

Now if you have a spouse or partner, and you want to successfully manage and spend money as a couple, then you have to navigate both of your values. And don't be surprised if you have some values that you share, and some that you don't.

It's not a problem – as long as you identify where you are aligned and where you're not when it comes to making decisions on your money and your life.

SARAH AND TIM

Sarah identified that she shared two of her top three values with her husband Tim: stimulation and achievement. The trick was that their number three value was poles apart. Sarah prized security while Tim loved free-spirited adventure (which fits under "hedonism" in the values on p20).

Tim had an old secondhand motorbike and loved to go for the occasional weekend ride. He was super excited when a friend invited him on a week of off-road riding in western NSW. Sarah was scared silly. His adventure-seeking clashed with her need for security. Tim, thinking that cost was the issue, assured her that the trip would be very low cost as he would ride his old bike.

In a world with no awareness of values, Sarah might have stopped him from going. Instead, Sarah asked the question: what can we do to enable you to go on your ride, without me worrying about whether you'll make it home in one piece?

The answer: Sarah and Tim agreed that they needed to spend the money to buy a better safer bike, more suited to the terrain.

1 HOW DO YOU IDENTIFY YOUR VALUES?

One of the most prominent theories on values is by Dr Shalom Schwartz – who has identified 10 universal values. These values are shown in the diagram below.

It's likely that you'll have some measure of each value, with some that resonate more strongly than others.

UNIVERSALISM Understanding, appreciation, tolerance and protection for the welfare of all people and for nature.	**POWER** Social status and prestige, control or dominance over people and resources.
BENEVOLENCE Preservation and enhancement of the welfare of people with whom one is in frequent personal contact.	**ACHIEVEMENT** Personal success through demonstrating competence according to social standards.
TRADITION Respect, commitment and acceptance of the customs and ideas that traditional culture or religion provide the self.	**HEDONISM** Pleasure and sensous gratification for oneself.
CONFORMITY Restraint of actions, inclinations and impulses likely to upset or harm others and violate social expectations or norms.	**STIMULATION** Excitement, novelty and challenge in life.
SECURITY Safety, harmony and stability of society, of relationships, and of self.	**SELF-DIRECTION** Independent thought and action – choosing, creating, exploring.

We recommend you take the quiz that Schwarz developed. Identify your top 3 values. And if you're in a couple, ask your other half to do the same. Then have a discussion to understand how they shape your common goals and priorities. And how they will shape your decision making as a couple.

Here's a link to a short version of the survey:
www.framevoicereport.org/media/1093/the-short-schwartzs-value-survey.pdf

2 GOALS

The second area is your goals. These are more time bound – and may change over time.

We recommend focusing on goals with a timeframe of up to five or 10 years. As humans, we're better at forming goals that are closer in time. We're good at setting goals for the next year or two, but after that it becomes a little fuzzier. And that's ok. You might set goals for five or 10 years out, but you might not end up pursuing them because they become less important, or the goal changes and initial goals are replaced by something that becomes more important to you.

Here's the work we recommend that you do

To understand your goals, we recommend that you use our worksheet. It's a model which is a little different to most. Here's how it works.

- Start by writing key points of context in the first row. Significant anniversaries or birthdays, key events or milestones. For example, you may have a child finishing school and starting university. Maybe you have a special birthday coming up or a special wedding anniversary or you might have a retirement or wind-down date for yourself or your partner.

- Now project 10 years into your future. Think about where you are. What you are doing. Who you are with.

- Next, identify your most important goals across the key goal areas – start by thinking 10 years out and working back in time.

- Finally, for each goal, write down the milestones that you need to achieve. So let's say I have a five-year goal of doing a luxury safari in Africa. What goals do I need to set for the two-year mark, the one-year mark, and in the next three months to have the best chance of achieving my five-year goal?

This should be fun. Create your map on a huge sheet of paper and pin it up on a wall and use multi-coloured post-it notes for your goals so you can move them around. Play with it.

GOALS	3 MONTHS	1 YEAR	2 YEARS	5 YEARS	10 YEARS
Big picture happenings in your world					
Personal					
Professional					
Financial					
Health					
Relationships / Family					
Community					

3 SET PRIORITIES

The third and final step is to create priorities.

As much as we might like to achieve all our dreams – sometimes we can't have all of them, or maybe just not all at once.

There may be some goals that are a clear priority over and above everything else. And there may be some goals that are less important and you're prepared to trade-off – which simply recognises that we don't have time and resources to do everything. This is even more the case where we are in a partnership, and we are trying to balance personal goals, our couple goals, and maybe our goals for our family.

The prioritisation process is about asking: how much money do I need to afford this goal – so it has a price tag; and how much time do I need to give to this goal.

Remember, you also have options

- You can push a goal out in time. So, the hiking holiday may need to wait for another year or two to allow for the home renovations.
- If a goal is too big a leap you can break it down into component parts. For example, with the home renovations in our example, you might just renovate a kitchen or bathroom and leave other things until later.
- You can re-shape a goal to still reach the heart of what you really want. For example, you might want to hike the Camino in Europe, but decide that you would be equally happy to hike the Three Capes in Tasmania.
- And there may be some goals that you decide are simply not a high enough priority for you to leave them in your planning.

	PRIORITY	BY WHEN
1	Setting up a monthly savings plan $4,000	August 2020
2	Renovate our house $20,000	Dec 2021
3	Hiking holiday	Feb 2023
4		
5		
6		
7		

This work is important because it helps us get a clear picture of the things that are most important to us, that will help us to fulfil our values and therefore help us feel purposeful and fulfilled in our lives.

It also then gives us the basis for building what our financial plan needs to look like in order to afford and achieve our priority goals.

Balancing your goals for your life now vs your future life

Often people seem to think that financial advisers exclusively think that the best use of money is to save it. And if you get to spend it, then that will be later. Sometimes much later.

It's true that we do focus on saving for the long term – whether that's major future goals like a sabbatical, helping the kids out with a kick start or your own retirement.

But we are also conscious that there are many opportunities to enjoy things today where you simply won't get that time or opportunity again. That might be a trip with an ageing loved one, holidays with young adult children (who soon enough may not want to holiday with you), or a new home that is a delight to live in and brings you joy each day.

So what's the answer? It's a delicate balance. Financial advice is not all about looking after your future self. It's also about creating joy for your current self.

The key element is to give real consideration to each decision. This is not about having or doing whatever you want. It is not about money mindlessness.

Do you defer repaying the mortgage to enjoy a family holiday skiing in Japan with your two teenage boys? That's what Kate did.

Do you turn down an offshore promotion that would pay a significantly higher salary because it would compromise the quality of life with your school age children? This is what one of Kate's clients did.

Do you buy a more expensive home that is open and tranquil even though you have to work two or three years longer to top up your retirement savings? Again, a decision by a colleague that has fallen into place is a source of daily delight.

Our view is that being money conscious is the ticket to occasionally being extravagant. A key part of the financial planning process is to capture all of these goals and priorities – for your present self and for your future self – and to create a plan so that you have the best chance of fulfilling those desires that for you are most important.

◢ QUICK STEPS

- Complete your values questionnaire and identify your top three. Have your partner do the same.
- Complete your goals worksheet.
- Complete your priorities worksheet.
- If you're part of a couple, take some time out and discuss what you've discovered.
- You might need a few rounds! Most of all, be open and make it fun.

2

BE "SASSY"

SASSY BY NAME, SASSY BY NATURE AND SASSY IN THE WAY WE CREATE THE STRUCTURE FOR YOU TO BE SMART WITH YOUR MONEY

R-E-S-P-E-C-T

Sassy is something we love – we aspire to be lively, bold, and full of spirit and a little bit cheeky.

SASSY is about creating a structure for you to be money smart – whether you're solo or in a couple.

SASSY STANDS FOR:

Spending – assess your current spending and create a cashflow plan

Assets and liabilities – assess your net wealth and create your target

Structure – create purposeful accounts and automate

Set rules and define triggers

Yearly review and weekly check-ins

Sisters are doing it for themselves

SPENDING AND CONSCIOUS CASHFLOW

We like the idea of managing cashflow. And one of our favourite ideas is "conscious cashflow".

Conscious cashflow is not about budgeting.

We dislike that budgeting has negative connotations around frugality and penny pinching and not spending.

We dislike that budgeting is often narrow in scope. It talks about expenses, without talking about the other side of the cashflow equation, which is income. While many personal finance experts focus on cutting expenses, we believe it is equally important to focus on finding ways to increase income.

And we dislike that budgeting is perceived to be something that poor people do. Some of Kate's wealthiest clients, who are exceptional money managers, still work to a disciplined budget. Hey, maybe that's one of the reasons they are wealthy?

So if cashflow is not budgeting, what is it?

Conscious cashflow is about ensuring that every time you spend money – for every single dollar that you spend – that you spend that dollar on something that aligns with your values, goals and priorities. This includes spending money to buy time (outsourcing things like chores) so that you can do the things that are most important to you.

It is about *maximising income* while minimising expenditure on stuff. Financial success comes from improving your career prospects and income earning ability without allowing increases in your standard of living to erode your gains.

It is about *knowing where your money is going,* how you are spending it (patterns of expenditure), and who you are spending it with (primary vendors).

It's about *spending less* while still getting what you value. This means when you spend money you make sure that you get a good deal. This is where negotiating comes in. Negotiating is a valuable money skill. Simply by asking your vendors for a discount can make a huge difference to your annual expenditure. And what's the worst that can happen? They say no. We find that the biggest challenge here is planning your purchases. Work out upfront what you need to buy, do your research to understand the product you really want, do research on pricing, be patient because patience enables you to wait for a sale.

It's about *limiting wastage* – the money that we spend on things that we don't really value. This might be lazy purchases, like buying a bottle of water when we could take a drink bottle from home (and save the environment). It can be buying clothing at a sale when we don't really need that item in our wardrobe, and haven't assessed what we really need.

It's about *identifying substitutes.* Let's say that you have a particular need. You've identified that it aligns with your values, goals and priorities. The question you can ask yourself is: what other ways could I meet the need? For example, you identify that you need a second car. You check out the models that meet your need. Then you shop around for the best price. But the question is: "Is there another way that you can resolve this need, without buying a car?" You could, for example, compare the price of buying a car with the price of using taxis. Or, you might evaluate whether you could use a ride-share to avoid all of the costs that come with owning the car. Price Go-Get, where you can access a car for specific periods of time – or a rental car where you need a vehicle for a longer period of time.

It's about **recognising a regular expense that is about to cease** – like daycare or school fees – and ensuring that you direct it smartly into savings.

HERE'S HOW TO BE MORE SASSY

Money – the best things in life are free – but you can give them to the birds and bees...

SPENDING

Start by assessing your current spending. We think one of the best tools available is the ASIC Smart Money Budget Planner. Simply download the excel spreadsheet from the ASIC website, and enter in your take-home income and your expenses. We like to use credit card and bank account statements to do this. It doesn't need to be correct to the cent – or even the dollar. The idea is simply to draw a picture of where your money is going.

Now you can benchmark.

People often ask what their spending should look like. This is a tricky one – as everyone's different.

Here is one useful rule of thumb:

- 50% on essentials – housing, utilities, food, essential clothing
- 30% on nice to haves – entertainment, special clothing, holidays
- 20% on savings

You might be thinking that you need a little more than 50% if you're living in a major capital city and paying a sizeable rent or mortgage. That's okay. You simply have to allocate some of your dollars for "nice to haves" into your allocation for "essentials". Just don't scrimp on the savings.

Now that you have a picture of your spending, and a benchmark to compare, the question you need to ask is this: What can I do to improve the way I spend money?

When you look at your cashflow and you're trying to find savings, our view is to look for the chunky money. We're not fans of necessarily focusing on cutting out your morning coffee. It really doesn't add up to that much on its own. If you enjoy your morning coffee, it's also probably not a sustainable change. Instead, look for the biggest ticket items – where does most of your money go? And who are the biggest suppliers – who do you spend most money with? Ask for a discount.

The main thing with conscious cashflow is you give things a whirl and you just keep practicing. We've found over the years that we just get better and better at not buying things we don't really need, at getting a better deal or finding substitutes mean that we don't need to spend as much money to achieve the same outcome.

If you're nearing retirement, you may find it helpful to check the analysis underlying the ASFA Retirement Standards – this shows the expenditure needed for a single or a couple to enjoy a comfortable or modest lifestyle in retirement. For home-owner couples, the annual cost of living is around $62k.

Create your cashflow plan

The next step is to create your future plan.

Back to the Smart Money Budget Planner (again). Though this time, you are going to use it to create your plan for how you intend to spend your money in the future.

Remember, this is about aligning how you spend every dollar to your values, goals, priorities. What changes can you make? What behaviours do you need to create to have the greatest chance of success?

Importantly, this includes not just spending but income. What are you earning? What is your income plan? What are your opportunities to negotiate a better income? What steps can you take (apply for a new role, seek promotion, improve your skills) to earn more?

> **PAY YOURSELF FIRST**
>
> Save first. Then you won't feel like you're failing at putting money away or that you've spent too much. Because the only money you've got left to spend is the money that's left over for spending. Automatically diverting money is a powerful tool! You can't spend what you can't see.

ASSETS AND LIABILITIES

This is about what you own and what you owe.

Write down your current assets (what you own) and liabilities or debts (what you owe). Also write down what the cost of your liabilities are (see pages 118-119 on how to calculate this).

Now, create a target plan.

What do you want your asset position to look like in 10, five, two and one year? Write your target for your assets and your liabilities.

Ask yourself: what changes will you commit to so that you have the best chance of achieving these goals?

Structure

This is about setting yourself up for the best chance of success.

We recommend structuring your money flow into five purposeful accounts – which align with the areas and benchmarks we discussed earlier:

- Essentials
- Nice to haves
- Savings – for the unexpected
- Savings – for fun
- Savings – for future you
- And we suggest that you split your savings 20/30/50.

So, of your savings:

- 20% to creating a buffer for unexpected expenses. This could be things like a major car repair, unexpected medical or health expenses, or an unplanned trip to visit ageing parents.
- 30% for fun. This is likely to include your short to medium term goals, whether it's travel, buying a new car, or throwing a great party.
- 50% for future you – which is your longer term savings, including additional contributions to super. More on this in Chapter 4 on super.

  Once you have our accounts set up, automate.

That means, setting up direct credits to each account to ensure that the money flows where you've designed it to flow.

And when it comes to savings, we're huge fans of the idea of "paying yourself first" – you treat your savings just like you treat rent or mortgage.

Most people spend first then save what's left over. Savvy savers flip that: save first then spend what's left over.

So, for example, if you have a goal around fast-tracking your loan repayments, then automate a payment so that this money immediately gets paid into your mortgage or offset account. Or if you have a goal to super-charge your retirement savings, make an auto contribution to super. And of course, you can do some of each.

The great thing about saving first is that it helps you succeed – without you having to do much at all. And that's because there's less risk that you'll beat yourself up for failing to put money away or feel guilty because you've spent too much. Because the only money you've got left to spend is the money that's left over for spending. So it's a powerful mechanism!

Set Rules

We're also fans for money happiness – and couple harmony – of pre-setting the money rules by which you will live. This applies if you're solo, or in a couple. You may even like to agree rules with your kids!

Here are some examples of money rules that you might like to try:

- Any expenditure from the "nice to have" account needs to be planned at least 30 days in advance.
- It's okay to spend money in the "nice to have" account without consultation.
- Any spend of $x or more needs to be discussed.
- Credit card debt is a no-go zone. Card balances are repaid every month.
- As a couple, we save equal amounts into our super funds each year.

You can also define trigger events to help you keep on track or plan for future events. Here's a few examples:

- Once we have $x in our "unexpected" savings account, we can re-direct 50% to our "fun" account and 50% to our "future you" account.
- When our mortgage is down to $x, we will make after-tax contributions to super.
- We will not spend on "nice to have" home renovations until our mortgage is $x.

YEARLY REVIEW

Our final sassy tip is to ensure that you undertake a full and thorough yearly review. Don't be on autopilot. Start at the top and review your values, goals and priorities, and then work your way back through the sassy framework.

Ask yourself these questions:

- What are we most proud of having achieved with our money management in the last year?
- What are we doing that's working well (and we want to keep doing)?
- What opportunities are there for us to improve?

And along the way, we recommend regular quick weekly check-ins to make sure you're on track. Importantly, these are about your life – not just money – because at the end of the day, the aim of good money management is to ensure that you create a great life.

KATE'S STORY

I had a goal of skiing in Japan. To keep this within my overall annual budget, I needed to identify other expenses on which I could save to effectively pay for the trip. This is the principle of ensuring that my spending doesn't keep growing with each new goal – and instead, that I am constantly managing my cashflow.

So, I checked all my annual expenses. At the time, one of my biggest ticket items (outside of my kids' education) was my yoga subscription. I paid over $1,600 a year for my yoga classes. While I could justify the cost on the basis that my cost per class was low, it was still a big chunk of money.

- I stopped going to a yoga studio, took up walking as my primary exercise – which is pretty much free – and then practiced yoga mostly at home.
- I started to stretch my hair cuts – so that instead of getting a hair cut every 8 weeks I had a cut every 12 weeks.
- I stopped my subscriptions to financial media and relied on online sources.
- I pared back my clothing expenses.
- We only dined out for very special occasions, and instead hosted friends at our place. We found we ate better food and drank far better wine!
- We looked at our alcohol bill – and I'm not a big drinker – but boy did it add up. We reduced how much we were buying and identified a better way to buy good wine online.

An important point here is balancing the budget. Just because you want to do something new, doesn't mean it makes sense to add it on top of your existing spend. What we've found works for us, is to plan our annual cashflow, and then if we identify an additional priority spend in the mix, then we need to do it within our existing budget. Which means that we have to make trade-offs to achieve a new goal or do something new.

For many years we made trade-offs around our holidays. We had annual two-week beach holidays with our kids and we camped. Even now we have an annual holiday at Easter, and go to Bluesfest. We made the decision to go camping because then we can have a week's holiday within our budget.

QUICK SAVING TIPS THAT DON'T HURT!

- Slow down the purchase process. It will help you to avoid impulse buying. Use the 30-day rule (#33 of the 50 top tips on p40) and if you can't wait that long, at least sleep on it.
- Stretch out timeframes – defer your renovations or buying a new car for another year or two.
- Buy depreciating assets second hand or demo. It's said that cars lose 25% of their value as soon as you drive them out of the showroom. Even with sporting equipment such as snow skis, demo skis sell at around 60% of the price of new.

It's fluid. Keep trying new ideas.

QUICK STEPS

- Pay yourself first. Set aside a target amount of savings then you can spend what's left.
- Structure your savings accounts. Set up three dedicated savings accounts. Have your salary paid into your main account and then set up automated direct debits into the other two so you don't need to think about it.

  1 Put 20% of your take home pay into this account.

  2 Put 30% into your 'fun' account.

  3 Leave 50% in your main account – this is the one you will use for your day to day living expenses. If you have money left over, put it into savings.

- Set rules that you'll live by.
- Be creative about finding ways to make your money go further. Read our section on 'feeling frugal' (see pages 38-41) for tips on boosting your savings and still enjoying life.

FEELING FRUGAL

TIPS TO BE FINANCIALLY FIT

If you're like me, your parents were careful about money – finding ways to stretch every dollar. Re-using, repairing, recycling and repurposing.

If you're ready to embrace being a little more frugal to be more financially fit, these are good ideas to resurrect – plus more.

Firstly, I seem to have inherited part of the frugal or post-war psyche from my parents. I often think in feast or famine terms and so like to put things aside for a rainy day. Unfortunately it's not money or savings, but an extra pair of shoes, dress, handbag, pair of earrings or stack of books.

I know I need to change that thinking. If I don't stop spending, I will never be able to afford to stop work.

Secondly, this has led to a lot of hoarding and cluttering which I know could make me some money if I sold it. The thought of selling at a loss has put me off for a long time – but keeping things for no reason is also unprofitable.

So maybe this is another area to flip my thinking.

Thirdly, we all need to think about working together to make society and our environment better. In the words of US singer and social activist Pete Seeger, we should be thinking: If it can't be reduced, reused, repaired, rebuilt, refurbished, refinished, resold, recycled or composted then it should be restricted, redesigned or removed from production. If we keep buying then we keep up production. It's up to us. What do we need? I know I need to focus on that question more closely, and more honestly. This change in thinking can change more than just my life. And when I look back, these are lessons my parents really taught by example. I need to remember those lessons better.

- *Julia*

HERE ARE OUR 50 TOP TIPS FOR SPENDING WELL AND SAVING WELL.

1. Install energy-efficient light bulbs. It will cut your electricity bill and you won't need to change them for a longer time than normal bulbs.

2. Turn off lights, heaters, air-conditioners when you're not using them.

3. Invest in a smart thermostat to regulate heating and cooling when you're not home to save money.

4. Check your insulation. You could be losing heat or cooling power that you're paying for.

5. Close blinds to help insulate your home. Close doors to rooms that you're not using.

6. Set your thermostat a little higher when cooling and a little lower when heating. Even a small change in the temperature can save you a lot of money.

7. Negotiate with your utility and services providers.

8. Find out what benefits your company offers. Do they offer staff discounts?

9. Cut or trim your viewing services – just stick with the ones you really enjoy.

10. Write a meal planner before you shop. Take out your diary and figure out how many meals and for how many people your family needs to cook for the week.

11. Write a shopping list and only buy what's on it. Just a few extra things can quickly add up to a lot more money.

12. When food is nearing its use-by date, relocate it to a special container in your fridge or your cupboard. Then find ways to use it in your meals.

13. Engage the kids in cooking dinner. Kate found that this made a big difference to them eating their meal without complaints as they'd contributed to making it.

14. Instead of buying take-away, try pre-packed spice kits or meal kits. This also helps make it easy for the whole family to help cook – or even be chief chef for a night.

15. Prepare more food from scratch. Kate bakes to relax and her family enjoys healthier treats than most things from a production line. It is usually cheaper, and always fresher and healthier.

16. Recycle glass jars – they're great for storing roasted tomatoes for your own pasta sauces, homemade jams, or preserved lemons.

17. Find the cheapest grocery stores, fruit shop, butcher, fish shop. Many people shop at big brand name outlets for convenience. Yet rarely are they getting the best deal. Kate switched to a different grocery store and automatically saved more than one-quarter on her shopping bill.

18. Entertain at home. Invite friends over and enjoy.

19. Start a garden, even if it's just a bunch of pots with your favourite herbs or berries.

20. Drink more water. Refill your own reusable bottle. You'll spend less on drinks, improve your health and contribute to the planet.

21. Take your lunch. The best way to do this is to deliberately plan to have leftovers from your evening meal and then before you serve dinner, pack your lunch for the next day. Even a few times a week can make a big difference.

22. If you do buy lunch or coffee then layer up the value. Rather than take-away, dine in at a nice café. Even better, sit in the sun. Even better again, invite a friend.

23. Get your kids to pack their own lunch. The more they can choose things they enjoy, the less likely they'll pressure you for a canteen order.

24. Don't spend big to entertain your kids. Head to the park or the beach. Hire a tennis court. Go to the local pool. Buy them canvases and paints. Get out in the garden. Visit a museum. Ride a bike. Walk around an interesting area or over an iconic bridge.

25. Mix up your holidays. Camping is a fantastic option to get away from it all and you can even hire camper trailers and all the gear.

26. BYO food for sports games and road trips. It makes it easier to find somewhere enjoyable to eat, and again you'll usually eat better and you'll spend less.

27. Don't shop to de-stress. Instead meditate, exercise, read, watch a movie, walk the dog, bake a cake. It's easy to justify spending to wind down, but it's rarely an emotionally or financially fit win.

28. Avoid shopping centres for entertainment. They're packed with temptation – so take the same approach as grocery shopping. Write a list of what you need, and work only from your list.

29. Clean out your wardrobe and only keep the things that you need or bring you joy. You may be able to earn some extra cash selling good clothes online, or simply give them away.

30. Declutter your cupboards. Work out what you really need and get rid of what's left.

31. Buy good quality appliances and devices the first time, and only buy what you need, when you need it. Research to find items that are well-rated and energy-efficient. It can save you significant money over time.

32. Service your appliances. Check online for service guides. Kate's husband has restored three expensive coffee machines she would otherwise have thrown away. Look after appliances and devices, they'll run more efficiently and last longer.

33. Apply the 30 day rule. This is designed to reduce impulse buying. Anything that you think you would like to buy you write down in a note. You then have to wait 30 days before you can buy it. Guess what happens? Most of the time, the impulse passes.

34. Buy on sale. Even better, buy at warehouse sales. But only if you need something. If you buy something on sale that you don't really need and it wasn't on your 30 day list then it was never really on sale.

35. Calculate the true cost of what you're buying. If you buy on your credit card and don't pay it off in the interest free period, whatever you have bought has an added charge each month until you pay it off.

36. With clothes, avoid buying for a single season. Buy to last.

37. Don't buy in bulk. Do you have time to wear more than 20 dresses each year? Or 10 new pairs of shoes? Do you really need new active wear for your yoga class? Cut back a little, or if you're like Julia, maybe a lot.

38. Repair clothes. Learn to hem, sew on a button, repair a tear.

39. For more serious re-fitting or re-juvenating, use a dressmaker. Take in or out clothes when you change shape. Re-fashion dated pieces.

40. Use public transport or walk when you can. Driving, parking and tolls can be expensive and not good for the planet.

41. Avoid fines. Speeding and parking fines are annoying and a waste of money.

42. Join a library instead of buying books. Online libraries are convenient and easy to use.

43. Share your books. Join forces with friends and share a good book around. We both like to support writers by buying books, and sharing them satisfies that and also gives them greater readership.

44. Reuse tea leaves, coffee grounds and scraps on your garden.

45. Keep old sheets and towels for when needed in the garden, shed or car. Old doonas make great dog beds.

46. Buy second hand. There are so many online market places and you can often find many things you need at a fraction of the price of something new.

47. When it comes to buying gifts for friends, weigh up whether they really need more material things. Can you instead enjoy lunch, dinner or a concert together?

48. Design and make cards and wrapping. It's fun and frugal.

49. Parents and elderly friends and relatives value time from you more than anything else. Consider this in the gift giving for them.

50. Continue little indulgences. If flowers are your thing let them bring you pleasure, if it's a magazine subscription, keep it. Just be mindful about what gives you pleasure and what savings you'll need to give you pleasure in the future.

3

INVESTING:
TAKING CHARGE
OF YOUR FUTURE

ONCE YOU UNDERSTAND THE CONCEPTS OF THE DIFFERENT ASSET CLASSES AND INVESTMENT VEHICLES, YOU ARE READY TO MAKE YOUR OWN INVESTMENT CHOICES

MONEY MONEY MONEY, ALWAYS SUNNY, IN A RICH MAN'S WORLD

Investing can be intimidating with its jargon, big numbers and fears of losing money – but it doesn't have to be.

The key is to have a plan. As one of the women we interviewed said: *"I spend a lot of time earning money and very little time investing it."*

Here, we step through the key elements of creating your individual investment plan.

STEP 1

SET YOUR FINANCIAL GOALS

We've talked about setting your personal goals – the things that are most important to you to achieve in life. These are important as they give the motivation – the "why" – for deferring spending now so that you can grow assets for the future.

Before you begin investing, you need to clarify the amount of money you need to save every month or year to give you the best chance of achieving your important goals.

Setting out specific financial goals is valuable because:

- You know what you're aiming for.
- You can easily track your financial progress and make changes if you're off track.
- It can help you to focus on your financial decisions and not be distracted by the latest shiny thing.

How to set financial goals

Go back to your goal setting exercise. Then, using a table like the one below, write:

• The amount of money you need.

• The time by which you need to have this amount saved.

Then calculate the final column with the help of ASIC's Smart Money savings goals calculator:

www.moneysmart.gov.au/tools-and-resources/calculators-and-apps/savings-goals-calculator

Ensure you consider inflation – or you may shoot for too low a number and miss out on your goal. When you're calculating the amount you need in future dollars, the amount needs to be higher than if you were calculating it in today's dollars. A simple way to adjust for inflation using the ASIC calculator is to reduce your expected annual return – so, if you assume an annual return of 5%, and inflation is estimated to be 2%, then your inflation-adjusted annual return would be 3%.

Here's an example. Catherine, age 52 has three key goals (shown in the table below) – and we can use the ASIC calculator to work out her monthly savings target. We will assume an annual return of 5% and inflation of 2%, so a real (inflation-adjusted) return of 3% a year.

The total monthly savings tells Catherine how much she needs to save for each time frame. Once she's achieved her holiday savings in eight years, she can tick that box – and reduce her monthly savings or re-direct into other goals.

GOALS	Total amount to save	Time frame	Amount to save each month – first 8 years	Amount to save each month – next 7 years
Holiday	$15,000	8 years	$138.10	$0
Repay mortgage	$150,000	15 years	$659.22	$659.22
Retirement	$300,000	15 years	$1,318.45	$1,318.45
TOTAL			$2,115.77	$1,977.67

STEP 2

START NOW– LEVERAGE THE POWER OF COMPOUNDING

Time after time

The amount of money you start with or save over time is often less important to achieving your financial goals as starting early.

One of the biggest mistakes people make is to procrastinate. They have good intentions of getting started, but then work or life – or simply not knowing where to start – gets in the way.

So they miss out on the leveraging power of compounding. Compound interest is like planting a big tree. A day shows no progress. A few years shows a little progress, 10 years is starting to look impressive, and 30 years can create something absolutely stunning.

WHAT IS COMPOUNDING?

In the simplest of terms, compounding interest means earning interest on interest. This means that every time interest is paid, it is paid on an increasingly larger amount that includes the previous interest earned.

Time is the compounding super-power – the more time you have on your side, the greater your investment dollars. Here's an example: 5% interest on $10,000 means you earn $500 interest. If you re-invest your interest, in the second year you earn interest on $10,500 – so now you've earned $525 and your balance has jumped to $11,025...and so on each year.

Here are the 5 key elements of compounding:

1. The rate of return

2. How often it is calculated (daily, monthly, quarterly, annually)

3. How much you add to your investments

4. How often you invest

5. The time span over which your money is invested.

Compound interest is like a snowball, which grows slowly at first, and then takes off as gains build on top of gains.

Here is a chart showing the growth of $10,000 over 30 years with monthly compounding and an annual real return of 5%:

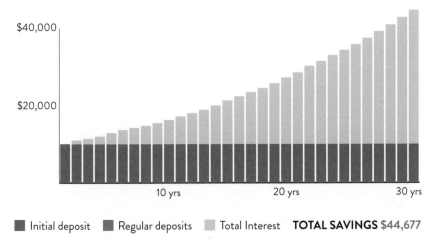

| Initial deposit | Regular deposits | Total Interest | **TOTAL SAVINGS** $44,677

You can see that in the first 10 years, the initial $10,000 grows to more than $16,000. Then, by 20 years, it has increased to more than $27,000. As the investment compounds, in the final 10 years, it is almost $45,000. And you haven't had to add a single extra cent: the heavy lifting has been done by compounding while you've sat back and relaxed.

Did you notice anything interesting in this example?
- The biggest impact is in the final 10 years.
- In 14 years the value of the investment has doubled. There's a neat rule of thumb called the "rule of 72" that you can use to work out how long it will take for your investment to double (see box on p48).

Now, this of course assumes that the annual returns are provided in a smooth manner – which is unlikely to be the case in real life. The reality is that some years you may have returns that are significantly higher than our assumed 5%, and some years you can have returns that are negative (more about this on p48).

Which brings us to a very important point. Compounding can only work for you if it is *uninterrupted*. You have to stick with your investment through good times and bad.

Now, you may be thinking: that's all fine. But I can't wait for 30 years to have stunning finances. That's okay. Starting now will give you the best chance of getting as close as you can.

If you're like many of the women we spoke to, you may feel like you don't know where to start.

The answer is, you can get started with very little dosh and a good savings habit. As we recommend in our sassy structure, put at least half of your 20% savings allocation from your net income (that's 10%) into *additional* mortgage repayments, *additional* super or investments.

THE RULE OF 72

This is an easy mental shortcut to help you estimate how long it might take to double your money. You simply take the number 72 and divide it by the annual rate of return. For example, an investment with a 7.2% compound annual rate of return will take 10 years to double in value. An investment with a 6% annual return will take 12 years; and if you were lucky enough to score a 8% annual rate of return, then you could double your money in 9 years.

This is pretty exciting stuff when you plug in all the potential numbers.

STEP 3

SAVE

She works hard for the money

Most investors spend a lot of time and energy on finding an investment which promises the best returns. Yet, investment returns can be elusive and hard won.

What if instead you could worry less about returns, and find something much more controllable to focus on?

You can! Saving at a higher rate usually has a bigger impact on your outcomes than higher investment returns, and with a whole lot less risk.

Let's assume Tom and Sarah are both 55, with a household income of $100,000 and only a few thousand in their super accounts. If they would like to retire by age 65 they have 10 years to play catch-up. If Tom and Sarah were to save 10% of their income and earn 8% on their investments, they would accumulate roughly $165,000 by the time they retire. Earning 8% per year would be helpful but may be difficult to pull off in the current environment of higher valuations and lower interest rates.

Now let's assume they instead save 20% of their income but only earn 4% on their investments. Under this scenario, they would end up with almost $275,000.

Savings really does the heavy lifting. It's worth repeating, saving really does the heavy lifting. It's the key to any positive financial advantage.

It's particularly valuable when you have a goal with a short to medium time horizon like this. Tom and Sarah's doubling of their savings rate leads to a far better outcome than doubling their investment returns.

And even better, this is with far less risk – you have complete control over how much you save, but no control over the performance of the markets.

HOW TO BE WEALTHY

Wealth comes from seven interrelated elements:

1. Your human capital – think of this as your earnings power. This includes what you're able to earn and your ability to work. It's based on your knowledge, skills and competencies – so it's important you invest in and nurture these.

2. Your regular savings – your ability to delay spending and convert part of your earnings into investments.

3. Your investments – your financial assets which you should expect to increase in value over time. The good news is that this work is done by your investments while you sleep!

4. Protecting your income – through personal insurances, so that illness or injury doesn't interrupt your earnings and savings.

5. Strategy and structuring – using careful planning to reduce the risk that your money is eroded by avoidable tax and your investments are designed for the right level of risk and a reasonable level of return.

6. Protecting your assets – through careful structuring to reduce the risk that your money is damaged by claims and life changes like divorce, remarriage or death. If you're like most people, you don't want assets ending up in limbo, or in the hands of someone you don't want to have them – instead keeping your money with the people you do want to have it.

7. Time – which is your lifetime and likely to be the most important driver of your wealth.

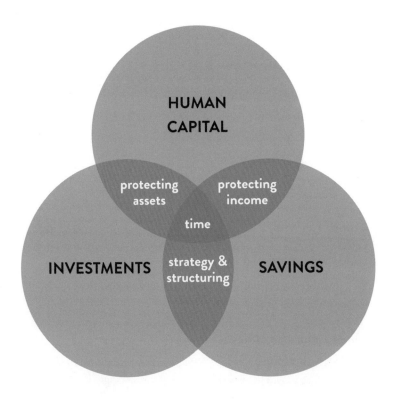

You'll see that time is right at the centre of our diagram. Here's why:

- The more time you devote to improving your earnings power – both in terms of the money you earn and the hours you work – the more money you have to increase your wealth.
- The longer you work, the longer you delay using your savings to live on – which means you have more money invested.
- The more time you have your money invested, the longer it can compound and grow.

STEP 4

START WITH YOUR RISK "BUDGET"

We believe it's essential when investing to start with your risk budget – rather than chasing returns.

Your risk budget is based on a few things:

- How long your money is likely to be invested.
- How bumpy a ride you can handle. We call this "journey" risk and it's about your ability to stay invested when your investments dive in value.
- How much you wish to grow your assets for the time you're investing. We call this "destination" risk and it's about having enough money when you need it to afford your goals.

Here's a guide to identifying your risk budget and how to create a mix of assets (or asset allocation) to match.

Determining your risk budget

There are many questions you can consider and questionnaires you can complete to assess your risk budget.

Here are just a few examples:

- Acknowledging that share markets can lose value in the short to medium term (this is the "journey" risk discussed above), how big a drop in the value of your investment could you stomach?
- How long will you invest your money? That is, when do you plan to sell your investments so you can use that money?
- How easily swayed are you by the investment opinions of non-professionals (friends, colleagues, the media)?

And it's certainly worth trying out some of the risk profile questionnaires available online – most super funds have a questionnaire, so give a few of them a whirl.

Rules of thumb abound here: An investment risk measure sometimes suggested is to take 100 (or 110, or 120) minus your age as the figure that should be in shares. However, we don't believe that your risk budget is primarily driven by your age. Instead, it needs to consider a range of factors – most importantly the 'sleep at night' test.

Having said that, we believe that there is one question that trumps all others. And that's our first question from the risk budget list.

If, however, an investor can ignore the media noise when investments drop sharply (which they do) they will be able to stick with them regardless. This investor is confident that their assets will recover over time and eventually be more valuable than they were before the dip.

If an individual is pummeled by the media noise and can't sleep at night, they'll want out. They'll sell – often at a low point – and that turns paper losses to permanent losses.

We call this the "sleep at night" test.

So here's our risk budget hack. Take a look at the table below, identify the depth of loss in your investments you could stomach in the short to medium term, and use that to guide your decision.

Worst return over any 12 months	-0.03%	-7.6%	-13.2%	-19.4%	-26.3%
What happens to $100,000	$99,970	$92,400	$86,800	$80,600	$73,700
Risk profile	Defensive	Conservative	Balanced	Growth	Aggressive

Source: Lonsec Research Pty Ltd. Period 31 Jan 2005 to 31 Jul 2019. Past performance is not a reliable indicator of future performance.

What we mean by these risk profiles

You'll often see terms used to describe risk profiles like "aggressive, growth, balanced, conservative". Here's what they typically mean.

	Invests in...	Historic annualised returns	Likelihood of a negative return (1 year in every x years)	This is for you if you...
Defensive	80% in cash like term deposits or highly rated bonds	5.68%	164	Want your money safe above all else. You would rather have a low rate of return than risk losing any money at all.
Conservative	40% in shares with 60% in bonds and cash	6.45%	10.3	Would like your investment money to have a smooth ride with only small bumps. You are comfortable to have an investment return that keeps you just ahead of inflation.
Balanced	60% in shares and 40% in bonds and cash	7.10%	8.2	Wish to achieve sound returns and can handle some moderate bumps in the short to medium term to achieve these long-term returns.
Growth	80% in shares and 20% in bonds and cash	7.67%	6.6	Would like a strong return on your investment, and can cope with a bumpy ride.
Aggressive	100% in shares	8.22%	5.1	Want the maximum return on your investment, and are willing to have a very bumpy ride.

Source: Lonsec Research Pty Ltd. Period 31 Jan 2005 to 31 Jul 2019. Past performance is not a reliable indicator of future performance.

There are two key conditions where the best option could be to stay safely in cash:

- You are unwilling to have any investment losses – even on paper.
- Your investment time horizon is less than three years.

Different funds may have different names for their portfolios and asset allocations may not be the same as ours. Read the fund's product disclosure statement to find out how money will be allocated for each investment option.

STEP 5

DIVERSIFICATION

Diversification in investments simply means having your money spread across a lot of different things. Ideally, you're spreading your investment money across completely different types of assets – cash, bonds, Australian shares, international shares.

The reasoning is easy – just because one of those things drops in value doesn't mean that the others will drop as far (or may even move in the opposite direction) so if you have your money spread across all of those things, you won't suffer if, say, the share market takes a dive.

Let's take a closer look at these different types of assets

The best way to think about different types of assets is in terms of their role in your portfolio:

• You need growth assets to increase your capital value and beat inflation
• And you need defensive assets to provide you with a steady hand when the going gets tough.

Think of it as being like a well-constructed band. You want to have charismatic, skilled musicians who are front and centre and interacting with the audience. But you don't want every band member front of stage. You also need rhythm and backing. Like your bass guitarist, keyboardist, drummer and backing vocalists.

It's the same in investing. Both the charismatic lead and backing musicians have a role in your strategic portfolio.

In the world of investing, the singer and lead guitarist types are the shares in your portfolio, and the backing musicians are the bonds.

WHAT ARE SHARES?

When you buy shares, you're buying a share of the company's assets and its profits. You're a part owner of the company.

Shares provide the best opportunity for growth over the long-term, so they'll build your wealth better than almost any other asset – as long as you can stay invested.

The flip side to shares' healthy long run return is that they carry risk, meaning that the price goes up but it can also go down. The main thing to remember is that if prices go down, and you don't need to use your money, then you can ignore the headlines and stay invested. It's useful to look at what the underlying companies are doing – rarely has their strategy or market position changed. You should have time for collective company share prices to make their way back up again.

The other thing to remember with shares is that even if their value goes down, they can still provide a significant proportion of total return as income. This means that, over time, your total return is positive, even though there will be times when your capital return is negative.

WHAT ARE BONDS?

When you buy a bond, you are providing a loan to a government or company. In effect, you are acting the same way a bank does when it loans a government money to enable it to build infrastructure or for a company to invest in new equipment or products.

Bonds offer a steady income. While they generally won't achieve the heady returns of shares in any given year, they also won't suffer the horrid lows.

Now, while that all sounds very logical, the trick is, being a diversified investor is hard.

- At any given time, you'll have an asset in your mix that gives you outstanding returns. You'll wonder why you didn't hold more of it.

- That asset can turn and bite you. You would have loved emerging market equities in 2017 with a 27.5% return. And you would have hated them as they fell 5% in 2018. You might not even remember loving it the year before.

- You will always hate something in your portfolio. If you don't, you're probably not well diversified.

- And because you have a mix of assets, your returns will always lag the best performing asset class. And you'll feel that you've missed out on returns. Maybe you have – but you've also missed out on risk.

Most people find it hard to stick with a diversified asset mix. Even when the markets are stable, they don't like sitting still – they want to fiddle and add a bit of this or reduce a bit of that. However, it doesn't make sense to change your investments based on market performance. When share markets go up and down, this is normal – this is exactly what they are expected to do.

If you have well considered diversified set of investments, it will serve you well in the long run. Allow diversification to do its work for you.

STEP 6

BUILDING A PORTFOLIO
THE ROLE OF MANAGED FUNDS AND ETFS

We like the idea of using pooled investments – like managed funds and exchange traded funds (ETFs) – rather than trying to trade direct shares. This is because these funds pool together many people's money and invest in a diversified range of investments, including shares and bonds. They can help you access investments that you couldn't easily or cost-effectively accesss yourself.

Managed funds

A professional fund manager determines how to invest the assets in the fund, selecting the company shares, bonds or other investments inwhich to invest. And rather than you owning the investment directly, the fund owns the investments and you are allocated units representing your share of the fund. The value of your units changes with the value of the underlying investments, which is reflected in the unit price.

Managed funds are helpful as they:

- Make diversification easy.
- Are simple to invest in and to make regular savings.
- Can provide you with a regular income stream.
- When it comes to tax time, provide you with tax reporting, making it easy to handle tax matters. (There is no point chasing fancy investments that complicate your tax.)

Exchange Traded Funds (ETFs)

An ETF is similar to a managed fund in that it is also a collective investment where many investors come together to invest in the one fund.

Typically, if the same investment manager has a managed fund and an ETF, it will hold similar underlying investments. The difference is an ETF can be traded on the Australian Securities Exchange (ASX).

Which is better?

We believe that neither is better – they're just different. You will need to open an account with a sharemarket broker to buy and sell ETFs. And check the cost – even though the headline cost of an ETF may appear cheaper than a managed fund, ETFs generally have higher trading (brokerage and buy/sell) costs, so the end cost may be the same.

Here are some things to consider:

- How much you have to invest. For most managed funds, you'll need a starting investment of $5,000 or $1,000 if you commit to a regular savings plan. With an ETF, you'll only need $500 to get started.
- How often you invest. Brokerage fees apply when buying ETFs on the share market, however, you don't pay brokerage when investing in a managed fund (though buy/sell spreads do apply). If you are going to make regular ongoing contributions, a managed fund will probably be a better option than an ETF.
- How quickly you want to trade. With managed funds, there is a trading window each day but ETFs are like shares that can trade at any time during the day. We believe that in most cases, investors shouldn't be trading like this anyway and so the added brokerage costs of investing in ETFs can make them less attractive than managed funds.

Managed funds are suited to investors who:	Exchange Traded Funds are suited to investors who:
Have $1,000 or more to start investing	Have $500 or more to start investing
Make regular ongoing investments	Make large, irregular investments
Are more likely to 'buy and hold' than regularly trade	Wish to trade throughout the day

How do you choose a fund?

Ignore the league tables of the best performers. It's not a good measure of whether an investment fund can offer consistently good returns over time.

One of the best rules of thumb is to find a fund that's low cost. Morningstar Research shows that the single biggest predictor of an investment fund's success is fees. Which is one reason why index funds may be a good option.

If you want to clarify the impact of fees on your investment, then try this calculator from ASIC Money Smart:

www.moneysmart.gov.au/tools-and-resources/calculators-and-apps/ managed-funds-fee-calculator

We've found this handy set of tools provided by Vanguard Australia which includes three helpful calculators:

• A fund comparison
• A managed funds fee comparison calculator
• An ETF fee comparison calculator

www.vanguardinvestments.com.au/retail/ret/investor-resources/ learning/calculators.jsp

We're not making a recommendation that you invest with Vanguard, that would depend on your personal circumstances and investment goals, but we are recommending their tools to help you make an informed investment decision.

STEP 7

TRACK YOUR PERFORMANCE AND PERIODICALLY REBALANCE

When you invest, even though your focus is on the long run, you need to keep tabs on what's going on, and you should adjust when necessary.

If you're diversified into different assets, some of those will have better returns than others over time. Which is why you may need to rebalance.

As part of your yearly review, check your investments and see if you need to rebalance. Let's say your shares have increased in value and are now 10% more than your risk budget suggests. That could be a good trigger to rebalance.

How do you rebalance? It simply comes down to moving your investments so that they stay in line with the amounts you set for your investment risk budget at the start.

For example, let's say you want to have 60% shares and 40% bonds in your portfolio. Two years later, shares have performed strongly and the mix has changed to 70% shares and 30% bonds. You could sell 10% of the value of your shares and invest this amount in bonds. A couple of years after that, your assets have changed again – shares have lost value and you have 50% shares and 50% bonds. In this case, you could sell 10% of the value of the bonds and use this money to buy more shares.

You can rebalance in one of two ways:

- The best option is to use new money to top up the assets that are underweight (so you don't need to sell any assets).
- Alternatively, you can sell some of the assets that you have too much of and put this money into the investments where you have a shortfall.

If you don't rebalance, you could find yourself wandering off track.

1. Lump sum vs dollar cost averaging

A common question for people with a lump sum to invest is: what can I do to avoid buying an investment and then have the market take a dive?

The answer is this: there is no perfect time to invest. You can't wait until markets are less uncertain because they will always feel uncertain. But there is one option which, while it may not improve your returns, certainly can help spread your risks and help you sleep at night. And that's to make periodic investments – also known as 'dollar cost averaging'.

Dollar cost averaging simply involves investing your money in stages – regardless of what's going on with market prices. So, for example, if you had $100,000 to invest, you might invest $10,000 a month over 10 months.

While the research indicates that investing all your cash at once gives you a higher probability of enjoying larger gains, it also increases the chance that you'll experience larger losses. So, if you want to decrease market risk and sleep better at night, dollar cost averaging can give you a smoother ride and a lower probability of seeing large losses.

2. How to manage a windfall successfully

If you receive a huge windfall, put it in a short-term investment for six months and just think about it and plan carefully what you're going to do with it. Types of windfalls include inheritance, redundancy, financial settlement from divorce, compensation payment or a life insurance benefit. This is a situation where you really should have a professional help you, as you'll not only be dealing with a substantial money decision, you're also probably navigating a tricky emotional life change. From a money perspective, there are likely to be many strategic opportunities available to you.

3. Do you need an adviser?

In many cases, we would suggest the answer is yes. It's always a good idea to have an expert opinion when you're planning to make a big decision. Refer to Chapter 13 — on how to choose an adviser who is likely to be a good fit for you.

FINAL WORDS

Investing by nature requires some activity. But not much. While it's never completely hands off, investment markets rarely reward investors who are hyperactive.

The media always loves to hype things. They love to hit the panic button. They'll try to convince you that this or that investment is the hottest thing. The next, they'll tell you that the world is falling apart. Usually, neither one is true.

The media simply knows that hype and fear are the things that attract viewers and readers. If you take nothing from this chapter, ignore panicked media commentary and stay calm. Focus on the fundamentals – a diverse investment mix that matches your risk budget.

After all, this is your life, your goals, your money. And what could the commentators – no matter how smart they are – possibly know about all that? Instead we say: save appropriately, invest regularly, keep calm and ignore the lows and highs, only sell when you need cash and rock on.

 QUICK STEPS

- Write down your priority goals. How much money do you need by when?
- Calculate your monthly savings – use the tools we've highlighted. And remember, higher savings usually trump higher investment returns.
- Work out your risk budget – use our guidelines or try out an online risk profile tool.
- Pick a good-quality, low-cost investment fund that matches your risk budget.
- Set up automatic savings and start investing now.
- Stay focused on your goals – don't stray into the latest shiny investing thing or fear of a market downturn. This is likely to harm not help you achieve your dreams.

LET'S GET THIS PARTY STARTED

YOU WANT TO INVEST, BUT YOU'RE NOT SURE WHERE TO START?

Here are 5 ways to start investing

1. Decide if you'd like to DIY or buy a ready-made portfolio

If you're keen to select your own shares, then a good option is to find a broker or online broking service. If you would prefer to have a professional investment manager handle the choice of investments for you, then managed funds or exchange traded funds (ETFs) are likely to be your 'go to' option.

2. Open an account

A popular option, particularly if you are looking to DIY and want low fees, is to open an online broking account. You can use this to buy shares, ETFs and even some managed funds.

You can open an account through any of the major banks (which can be handy as you will need to link a cash account to your broking account to buy investments and receive payments).

To open an account you'll generally need to provide key personal details – including your name, address, date of birth, your tax file number and details of your bank account. It's usually a good idea to have a bank account specifically for your investments as it makes it easier when it comes to your records for tax time.

With an online brokerage account, you also need to set up how your shares are held. The easiest way is a broker Holder Identification Number (HIN) – a 10 digit number that begins with an "X" and represents all your share holdings at that broker. This makes it easy to trade instantly because your broker has the details for your exact holdings.

If you're looking for the 'ready made' fund option, it's likely to be easier to choose an investment manager and open an account directly with them. And you can get help from their client service staff to step you through the process.

3. Select the investments you would like to buy

You can select from any listed investments including more than 2,000 companies on the Australian Stock Exchange (ASX), more than 200 ETFs and more than 200 listed managed funds.

If you are keen to research and choose your own shares, ASIC MoneySmart suggests starting with companies in an industry that you know something about, as this may make it easier for you to understand how a business is doing.

If you feel more comfortable selecting a managed fund or ETF, then try this tool provided by Vanguard Investments: *https://tool.vanguardinvestments.com.au/mstar/au/fundcompare. htm##target=fct*

And don't think direct shares are better than funds – did you know that world-famous investor Warren Buffet has asked for his estate to be invested into index funds?

4. Transfer funds into your account

Whether you're opening an online brokerage account or investing directly with a fund manager, make sure you transfer enough money into the account to cover your investment purchases and any transaction costs.

5. Make sure you report on your investments at tax time

You need to report on any investment gains you've made (or losses) and all dividends or distributions that you've received – even if you elect to reinvest them.

Finally, remember that all investments involve risks – the good news is that you can manage this by doing your homework, investing in line with your comfort level and taking a long-term approach.

THE 57-YEAR ITCH

A few years ago I had a friend aged 57. He had a house which he owned outright, just outside Sydney. He'd bought it with the proceeds of the home he'd split with his wife in Sydney.

The home he'd bought had a decent rent, it was likely to see capital value, but it was a long term prospect. So a little panicked about his future, and the house not appreciating as quickly as he hoped, he thought he'd pick up and change his life by moving overseas to Bali and living cheaply. He was able to find cheap tickets, and a cheap place to live and was able to quickly start a new life. However, without good financial advice he didn't know the cost of being assessed as a non-resident. It's costly and ate away at the rent his property was earning and it cut the Bali dream short.

When I heard this I thought this was a knee jerk reaction to sorting finances pre-retirement. I was frustrated telling a colleague of mine about my friend and his lack of planning for his future and he said, this was common in people aged 57. Go figure!

There was actually a certain knee-jerk age at which people (mainly men*) suddenly realised that impending retirement was bearing down upon them and they knew they didn't have enough to live on in retirement so they started making desperate money moves. This included buying shares, investing in get-rich-quick schemes, that they hoped would pay off in the next few years. Inevitably, it usually ended up with them wasting money they saved which they could potentially have put to better use had they engaged professionals to help them manage their finances and their fears.

You have to be realistic – if you want to retire at a certain age with a certain amount of money to fund your lifestyle and you look like you're going to reach that age without that sum you have three main choices. Firstly, don't retire at that age, continue working until you are able to reach that amount, or secondly, decide that you will retire with the reduced amount of money and will have to downgrade the lifestyle you wanted in retirement, or finally, work out a compromise between the two.

If you think you're nearing retirement age and you're not sure if you're going to make it - seek advice

If you think you're nearing retirement age and you're not sure if you're going to make it, seek advice. Ask someone who is an expert to crunch your numbers for you and work out if there is a way to make it. A little extra saved, a diversion of income, or a number of other strategies might get you over the line.

Take charge today.

*women tend to be more risk averse

4

SUPERANNUATION
A FRIEND INDEED

SUPERANNUATION CAN BE
A GIFT IF YOU START EARLY
AND MAKE FULL USE OF THE
BENEFITS – THE PROBLEM
IS WE OFTEN FIND IT TOO
UNSEXY UNTIL IT'S TOO LATE

SUPERANNUATION YOUR TICKET TO COME WHAT MAY

MONEY FOR NOTHING

We know the mention of superannuation can be boring and we don't want you to stop reading – what we think more accurately describes what we are talking about is future freedom. It's the money to look out for your future self. The money you save now can help you make choices down the track such as leaving work earlier, being able to continue living your lifestyle even after you stop working and being able to afford things you might otherwise not have been able to do post-work.

The Australian Super system is an amazing system. It is confidently ranked third worldwide in terms of quality of pension systems, behind the Netherlands and Denmark. We're very fortunate to have a high quality and sustainable system with a forced savings element (in the form of super guarantee contributions) that helps us provide for our future self – and an income when we're no longer working.

The thing about super is that it's not an investment in itself – it's just a structure for your investments that is very attractive. Why? Because you save money through a framework that gives tax benefits. You can think about these tax benefits as being a reward for having your money locked away until your retirement.

It's not exactly money for nothing, but since most of us have employers paying superannuation on our behalf, it's money that's no sweat.

There is a raft of complex rules and regulations around superannuation. However, armed with some key information which we'll share in this chapter, you should be able to navigate the key elements of the super system confidently.

HOW DOES SUPER WORK?

We find the easiest way to describe how super works is to divide it into three parts: money in, money invested within, and money out.

MONEY IN

There are two main ways in which you can contribute money into super:

- Before tax – known as "concessional" contributions, and
- After tax – known as "non-concessional" contributions.

Concessional contributions

Concessional contributions are contributions made before tax. There are three key types:

- Employer super contributions – made for you by your employer (if you're eligible), as part of the Superannuation Guarantee (SG) scheme. The current rate is 9.5% of your salary (though this only needs to be paid up to a certain maximum contribution limit) and is expected to gradually rise to 12%.
- Salary sacrifice contributions – these are contributions which you elect to make by arranging for your employer to make a payment from your before-tax income.
- Tax-deductible personal contributions – these are contributions you can make from your own funds using after-tax dollars (eg. transferring money from your bank account into your super), on which you claim a tax deduction in your tax return. Self-employed people often use this type. Of course, you can only claim a deduction where you have taxable income that is more than the contribution amount. It is also important to note that there is a special form (a "notice of intent to claim or vary a deduction for personal super contributions" form) that you must complete and lodge with your super fund before the end of the next financial year or before completing your tax return (whichever comes first). Your super fund should acknowledge this in writing before you claim a deduction on your tax return.

There's currently a $25,000 limit on these concessional contributions into your super each year.

Until recently, this cap was reset every year – so if you didn't contribute the full $25,000 into your super you couldn't use any unused amount in future years. Now the super rules have changed, and you may be able to carry forward any unused amount for up to five years (see box p73).

From a tax perspective, while you don't pay income tax on these concessional contributions when they are received by your super fund, a 15% contributions tax applies. If you earn income of $250,000 or more a year, there is an additional 15% contributions tax payable (so 30% in total).

So, for example, if you contribute $100, the standard tax is $15 and $85 is invested in your super account. If you're a high-income earner, then the tax is $30 and $70 is the amount invested.

There is also a bonus for lower income earners – with a low income super tax offset of 15% (effectively negating the 15% contributions tax). You could be eligible if you earn $37,000 or less a year. In this case, you could receive a refund of the contributions tax up to a maximum of $500 per year. If you're eligible, the offset will be automatically deposited into your super account once you have lodged your tax return.

PLAYING SUPER CATCH UP

Can you make catch up concessional contributions?

- Is your total superannuation balance less than $500,000 on 30 June of the previous financial year?
- Are you younger than age 65 (or do you meet the work test if you're 65 to 69)?
- Do you have unused amounts of concessional contributions (commencing 1 July 2018)?

Here's a quick case study

Asha is self-employed and has $400,000 in her super account. For financial years 2019 and 2020, she has made concessional contributions of $5,000. Asha has an unused cap for each year of $20,000 – a total of $40,000. So, in financial year 2021, she could put in as much as $65,000 – that's her $25,000 cap plus her unused cap amounts from the previous three years. Asha makes a personal tax-deductible super contribution of $40,000 on top of her usual $5,000 contribution. She still has $20,000 in unused contributions that she can carry forward to the following year. However, Asha needs to be careful: if her extra contributions (and growth in her super fund) increase her super balance to more than the $500,000 threshold, she won't be able to use the unused concessional contribution amounts in future years. However, if this does happen, she can still carry forward her unused amounts for up to five years just in case her balance falls below $500,000 again.

	2018-19	2019-20	2020-21
Concessional cap	$25,000	$25,000	$25,000
Super contribution	$5,000	$5,000	$5,000
Top up concessional contributions	$0	$0	$40,000
Total concessional contributions	$5,000	$5,000	$45,000
Cumulative unused cap Asha can carry forward	$20,000	$40,000	$20,000

These catch up rules could be valuable for people who've had career breaks, started businesses, or are nearing retirement and want to maximise their super and manage their tax.

Non-concessional contributions

Non-concessional contributions refer to money you put into your super fund using after-tax dollars and for which you are not seeking to claim a tax deduction.

In this case, there is no contributions tax. If you put $100 in, then $100 is invested into your superannuation account.

There are limits on how much you can contribute to super as a non-concessional contribution. Each year you can contribute up to $100,000 as long as you meet the eligibility criteria (see box p67). If you're younger than age 65 (expected to change to age 67 from 1 July 2020), you may also be able to bring forward two future years of this cap, allowing you to contribute up to $300,000 at a time.

There is a threshold which may limit your non-concessional contributions. If your total super balance (which includes all super funds and any pension accounts) as at 30 June of the previous financial year is less than $1.4 million, then you can make the maximum contribution. On the other hand, if your individual total super balance is $1.6 million or more, you can't make any additional after-tax contributions to your super. And if your super balance is somewhere in between, then your maximum contribution might be one or two years' worth – as we've outlined in the table below.

Super balance	Max contribution amount under the bring forward rule	Max contribution amount using the bring forward rule
Less than $1.4m	3 x NCC cap	$300,000 (3 years)
$1.4m to <$1.5m	2 x NCC cap	$200,000 (2 years)
$1.5m to < $1.6m	1 x NCC cap	$100,000 (1 year)
$1.6m or more	Not eligible	$0

TOTAL SUPER BALANCE CASE STUDY

Mia is age 60 and has a super balance of $1.49 million at 30 June 2020. She hadn't made any non-concessional contributions in the last few years. As her total super balance was between $1.4 million and $1.5 million, she could contribute up to $200,000. Mia made a $150,000 non-concessional contribution into super in July 2021, which triggers the bring-forward rule (so she has a bring-forward amount of $50,000 left). In July 2022 Mia decides she'd like to contribute up her unused bring-forward amount of $50,000. However, her total superannuation balance is now $1.62 million. As this is more than the $1.6 million cap she can't make any more contributions.

The bring forward contribution is illustrated in the diagram below.

Above $1.6m = ineligible to make non-concession contributions

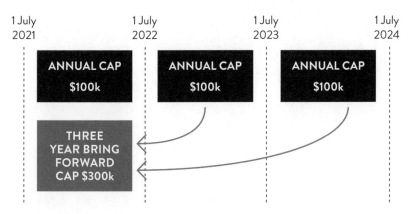

It's important to note that you need to be age 64 or younger to use the bring-forward rule. If you're in your 60s, you also need to keep in mind the age-based limits on contributing to super (see box page 76).

It's worth carefully planning your non-concessional contributions as an individual and as a couple (if partnered) to make the most of your caps.

BOOSTING YOUR SUPER IF YOU'RE 67 OR OVER

Once you're getting close to age 67 there is a range of age-based rules that determine if you will be able to contribute super – and these can change. So you do need to check the rules at the time you're ready to contribute.

There are special super rules for anyone aged 67 and over. If you're working, you can continue to receive Super Guarantee employer contributions and can make personal concessional (pre-tax) or after-tax super contributions up to age 75 if you meet the work test or work test exemption. Once you reach age 75, you're generally not able to make voluntary contributions into your super (except for the downsizer contribution – see p77).

To meet the **work test**, you must have been gainfully employed (that is, in paid work) any time during the financial year for a minimum of 40 hours within 30 consecutive days.

To meet the **work test exemption,** you must:

- Have met the work test in the previous financial year
- Not have been, nor intend to be, gainfully employed for at least 40 hours within 30 consecutive days in the financial year in which the contributions are made
- Have a total superannuation balance (across all super accounts) of less than $300,000 at 30 June of the previous financial year, and
- Have not previously made contributions to super using the work test exemption.

In each case, your super fund will ask you to complete a declaration each year to confirm that you meet the work test or work test exemption requirements.

Spouse contributions

Spouse contributions are a special type of non-concessional contribution – where a spouse may receive a tax offset for contributing on behalf of their partner if they're eligible. This requires that the spouse:

- Is younger than age 67, or if aged 67 and can meet the work test or work test exemption.
- Earns income of less than $37,000 for the full offset or between $37,000 and $40,000 for a partial offset.

These figures are indexed each year and can change. The offset is 18% tax offset on an amount of up to $3,000 (that is, $540). Again, you need to include this when completing your tax return at the end of the financial year.

Other ways to get money into super

Co-contributions: You may be eligible for a government co-contribution of up to $500 if you make an after-tax contribution to your super, for which you haven't claimed a tax deduction; and your income is less than $53,564. These figures are indexed each year and can change.

You don't need to apply for the super co-contribution, simply provide your tax file number to your super fund. Once you've lodged your tax return, the Australian Taxation Office (ATO) will work out what you're eligible to receive and any co-contribution should then be deposited into your super account.

Downsizer contributions: If you sell your home and are aged 65 or older you could put up to $300,000 (for each individual) from the sale into super. The good news is that there are no contribution or age-based limits, and your work status, superannuation balance, and contributions history don't matter. There are eligibility rules including that you have owned your home for at least 10 years, and it has been your main residence.

Splitting your super concessional contributions with a spouse: this may make sense if you want to boost your partner's superannuation balance.

Splitting your super concessional contributions with a spouse: this may make sense if you want to boost your partner's superannuation balance. It is only concessional (pre-tax) contributions that can be split, and it is only the amount after the 15% contributions tax is deducted (so if you split a $10,000 concessional contribution, $8,500 can be transferred to your partner). The contribution is still counted towards the contributing spouse's contribution cap. As with all things super, you need to check that your super funds will allow super splitting, and to check the eligibility rules.

CHECK YOUR SUPERANNUATION IS BEING PAID

While you might not think about your super like you do your income, it's a good idea to check that the money is being correctly paid – and into the right account. If your employer were to become bankrupt it could be hard to recoup this money. Remember, it's your money – keep a close eye on it.

MONEY INVESTED IN SUPER

Now you may be thinking: why would I put my money into super when I can't access it until age 65 or retirement?

The answer relates to your earnings and growth within super. Any investment grows by earning income – when dividends or distributions are paid – and by your assets growing in value.

The advantage within super is that your money enjoys a low tax rate – a maximum of 15% on income earned and 10% on capital gains. That compares with investments you own where tax could be up to 45% (excluding the medicare levy). This low tax rate is even more attractive when you think about the benefits of compounding of returns over time.

The chart below shows the difference super makes. It shows the average annual returns for Australian equities for the 10 years and 20 years to 31 December 2017 – including the impact of tax. The blue bar is the gross return – that is, before any tax is deducted. The red bar is superannuation and the lilac bar is for an individual investor at the top marginal tax rate.

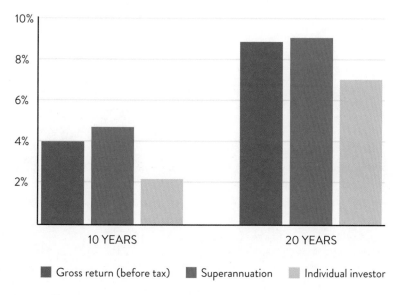

Gross return (before tax)   Superannuation   Individual investor

Source: Russell Long Term Investing Report 2018

You can see that the individual investor loses around 1.4% to 2% in average annual returns in tax. And you've probably noticed that the super fund investor actually does a little better than the gross return – thanks to the magic of franking credits (see box p80).

YOUR SUPER INVESTMENT RETURN INCLUDES THREE PARTS:

Income: Is the return from such things as interest payments, share dividends, or managed fund distributions. If you think of it in terms of a property, this is like rental income. In super, this income is taxed at 15%.

Capital growth: This is the increase in the value of an asset. You might buy shares in a company at $4, and a year later they're worth $6. Your capital growth is $2. Now, if you sell the shares you may have a capital gain. On the other hand, your shares could decline in value. Let's say your $4 shares drop in price to $3 – now you have a capital loss of $1. It's important to remember that until the time that you sell your shares, any capital gain (or loss) is only on paper – the tax impact is only when you sell. In super, as long as you've held the asset for at least 12 months, any capital gain is taxed at 10%.

Franking credits: These are tax credits that may come with dividends paid on Australian shares. They are designed to offset the income tax paid by the company (approximately 30%). The idea is that the investor should pay their own individual rate of tax on the dividend, and avoid double taxation (i.e. paying tax twice on the same income). Because the rate of income tax for a super fund (15%) is currently below the company tax rate super fund members may receive a tax credit – which helps to boost their overall returns.

MONEY OUT

The third part of the super story is drawing money out. So, this is when you ultimately wind down or retire and you want your super savings to provide you with income.

When can you access your super?

The earliest you can typically access your super is at your "preservation age" (which refers not to you but to your money, which has been happily preserved and working for you in your super account). Your preservation age is currently between 55 and 60, depending on when you were born.

WHAT IS YOUR PRESERVATION AGE?

DATE OF BIRTH	PRESERVATION AGE
Before 1 July 1960	55
1 July 1960 to 30 June 1961	56
1 July 1961 to 30 June 1962	57
1 July 1962 to 30 June 1963	58
1 July 1963 to 30 June 1964	59
1 July 1964 and onward	60

Here is the fine print on when you can access your super:

- When you reach preservation age and retire.
- If you're aged 60 to 64 and stop working (for any amount of time). This is the case even if you are not intending to retire completely. This means you can draw on your super, even if you re-commence work under a different employment arrangement or a new company.
- When you turn 65, regardless of whether you're working or not.

ACCESSING SUPER EARLY

Generally, superannuation is designed to be preserved until retirement, apart from the special conditions for contributors to the First Home Super Saver Scheme.

However, there are cases where you may be able to access super early, for example, in the case of severe financial hardship, or suffering certain medical conditions. You would need to check with your super fund to see if you meet the eligibility criteria.

NAME
ANNE

ROLE
UNIVERSITY PROFESSOR

AGE 52

INCOME BRACKET
$150,000-180,000

RELATIONSHIP SITUATION
SINGLE, FULL-TIME PARENT

SUPER BALANCE
$635,515

OTHER INVESTMENTS
NONE

FINANCIAL ADVISER
NO

PROFILE

ESTIMATED PERCENTAGE OF INCOME YOU CURRENTLY SAVE

None at the moment – normally $200 per fortnight for holidays/extra expenses.

DESIRED AGE OF RETIREMENT

65-67

DESIRED RETIREMENT (WHAT YOU WOULD LIKE LIFESTYLE WISE)

Mix of travel, low-key activities/groups and time with my children/grandchildren. I don't think I will be ever fully disconnected from the intellectual world of my work but I do hope to fully retire and be free of admin/teaching by 65/67 or even before. After I retire I still hope to be attending events, providing advice where needed, reading material in my field but also some additional paid work in the form of reviews/writing/assessing manuscripts etc (though I don't envisage this to be a huge income stream).

WHAT IS YOUR CURRENT JOB, HOME AND LIFESTYLE SITUATION

I'm a university Professor, currently renting but looking to buy a home. I have primary care of a son who has just started high school; lifestyle is busy with lots of work/family commitments. Work includes a lot of travel. I aim for a decent work/life balance but I also love the work I do so sometimes I am happy to spend my weekends working. At the moment most of my socialising is done at work and with my two sons although friends are important to me and I love to spend time with them when I can.

WHAT YOU'D LIKE TO BE DOING NOW/ IN THE NEXT 5 YEARS/ IN 10 YEARS/ BEYOND

I am just really hitting my stride in terms of my career although moving interstate to a new city and becoming a single parent has been overwhelming at times. I hope to continue to build my career here and overseas. Perhaps move into a senior admin role in the final stages of my career to boost my income/savings/super and to give back to my profession through leadership.

I hope to enjoy a fairly active retirement, still connected to my scholarly community and activities but with time for other interests. I hope I have enough funds to lead a sociable life, travel, and help support my children as they enter different stages of their careers/lives.

HOW YOU'RE PLANNING ON REACHING THERE

Continue by being fairly strategic in terms of where I buy a home and also once I have bought a family home, think about an investment property.

CURRENT PRIORITIES

Continue to settle in to a new city/job and look for a home to buy.

FINANCIAL DECISIONS YOU'VE ALREADY MADE IN LIFE TO HELP YOU ACHIEVE YOUR GOALS

I haven't really consciously made financial decisions or had formal goals although I've been careful about the property (primary residence) I buy/plan to buy in terms of thinking about its long-term value. I've been fairly cautious with my Super having it in a low-risk Sustainable Balanced investment portfolio, which seems to have paid off so far. I've contemplated buying an investment property to help with retirement and having something for my children.

FINANCIAL SITUATIONS THAT HAVE AFFECTED YOUR GOALS TO DATE

I moved interstate at the end of last year for three reasons: career, payrise/promotion, new opportunities to develop research capacity and mentor research groups/people. My previous role didn't provide these opportunities. In my current role I hope to provide research leadership, develop projects, and publish my own work.

However, moving interstate feels like it has set me back financially but long term it will be more sustainable career-wise. Having children is of course the biggest financial setback for a lot of women, and especially as a single parent but I also realise I'm very lucky to be working in a relatively stable profession, although I've had to work incredibly hard.

OTHER COMMENTS

I have a generous Super scheme so this has made financial decisions easier. Working at a University provides a 17% employer contribution to Super.

I hope I have enough funds to lead a sociable life, travel, and help support my children

Drawing money out of super: commencing an account-based pension

When it's time to use the money you've been saving to super, you have two main options: you can withdraw it as a lump sum, or you can start an account-based pension.

The most common option is to use an account-based pension as it's a way of paying yourself a regular income – like the regular income you may have received when you were working. In fact, this is a great way to set up a pension – as a regular payment into your bank accounts (for example, with one for living expenses and one for major expenses).

One of the greatest benefits of an account-based pension – apart from the regular income – is that once you're age 60 it is completely tax free. That's attractive.

There are important rules around this no-tax status:

- Each individual can only transfer $1.6 million into an account-based pension (known as the "transfer balance cap")
- On commencing a pension, you must withdraw a minimum amount each year – which is a percentage of your account balance at 30 June of the prior financial year. This starts at 4% for individuals up to age 64, increases to 5% at age 65 and then continues to notch up at older age brackets. It can be paid regularly (eg. monthly) or as a single lump sum. It needs to be withdrawn each year regardless of whether investment markets are rising or falling.

Importantly, the only way that you can create a pension is from the money that has already been contributed to super. Which reinforces the importance of careful planning to add money to your super over time – and not leaving it until the 11th hour.

THE $1.6 MILLION TRANSFER BALANCE CAP

The transfer balance cap is a limit on the total amount of money that an individual can transfer from their super into what is known as the "retirement phase" of superannuation – such as an account-based pension. The way that the cap is calculated and managed is complex, and there are penalties for exceeding the cap, so it is a good idea to seek financial advice.

Combining your super

Combining your super accounts into one (also known as "consolidating") has some benefits. It can make it easier for you to keep track of your investments and it could save you in fees and charges.

However, there may be drawbacks:

- You could lose valuable insurance cover. It's always a good idea to clarify what insurance you need, and make sure that if you are going to close a super fund with insurance that you replace your insurance cover first.
- You may need to pay capital gains tax.
- If you mix a tax-free fund with a taxable fund you could lose some long term estate planning benefits.

As with all things super, it is often more complex than it may seem, and it is valuable to get advice.

HOW DO I COMBINE MY SUPER?

1. Locate all your super accounts: Gather your super statements and note the account values and any insurance held within each fund.

2. Find lost super: If you don't already have one, create a myGov account at www.my.gov.au, then link the ATO to your account. Go to the ATO section, select the "Super" tab and in this section, you can see details of all your super accounts, including any you may have forgotten.

3. Assess your insurance cover: identify what insurances you need, and then decide if you need to keep an existing fund open to retain the insurance, or if you will replace your insurance cover in your new fund. We always recommend arranging your new insurance before cancelling any existing insurance cover that you wish to retain. This may mean opening your new super fund and deferring a transfer from your old fund until the new insurance cover is confirmed.

4. Select your ideal new super fund: This may be one of your existing funds – or a completely new fund. You can use a super comparison tool to help you decide which fund is likely to be best for you (see box on p88).

5. Arrange for your new super fund to request the transfer of your old super accounts: Most super funds will happily do the legwork to transfer (rollover) your old super accounts into their fund. Simply tell them you wish to rollover, complete the relevant form (usually online), and sit back as they do the rest.

6. Arrange your employer contributions to be paid into your new super account: You will need to provide your employer with a "super choice" form which your super fund can assist you with. And if in future you change employers, make sure you give them details of your fund using a "super choice" form.

SELF MANAGED SUPER FUNDS

Many people choose to set up a Self Managed Super Fund (SMSF) because they want to take personal control of their superannuation.

An SMSF is a private superannuation fund, that you manage yourself. It has a limited number of members and all members must be trustees (or directors, if there is a corporate trustee). The trustees are responsible for decisions made about the fund and compliance with relevant laws.

While the control of your investment may be appealing, there are complex rules and restrictions with superannuation, and you have to be diligent and be willing to keep on top of the relevant paperwork. Even though you can outsource many of the activities to a professional administrator or accountant, you still need to understand your legal responsibilities and the investments you make because you are still responsible for your fund. There are set up costs – typically around $1,500 to $2,000 – and annual expenses can be in the order of $1,500 to $3,000, so an SMSF is generally only cost-effective with a large balance.

The main reasons that it may make sense to have an SMSF include:

- You wish to own your business premises through your fund.
- You are seeking asset protection – as generally funds held within a SMSF are protected from creditors in the event of insolvency.
- You wish to invest in direct property and unlisted assets – particularly if you would like to pool your money with family members so you can buy a more expensive property you may not be able to afford alone.
- Your estate planning needs (that is transferring your super benefits when you die) are complex and you would like control and flexibility in how you direct your assets to your nominated beneficiaries.

ASIC (Australian Securities and Investments Commission) has recently released a fact sheet which suggests that if your balance is below $500,000, you should ask your adviser why an SMSF is the best option for you. According to ASIC, generally, balances under $500,000 have lower returns after expenses and tax.

HOW DO I CHOOSE A SUPER FUND?

An easy way to compare Super Funds is using a comparison tool. One useful tool is the ChantWest Apple Check which you can access directly through ChantWest for a small fee, or you can find it for free on certain super fund websites. The tool enables you to compare up to three super or pension funds out of a pool of more than 200 funds including:
- An overall star rating
- The asset mix for each investment option and how they have performed
- Total fees on the nominated balance and transaction fees
- For super, the types of insurance available – premiums and key features.

A good rule of thumb for assessing the cost of your super is that total fees should be no more than 1% p.a. of the value of your super balance.

A final word. While it may seem fashionable to have an SMSF, they are certainly not for everyone. A mistake in running your SMSF could mean that your fund doesn't receive its usual tax concessions and ends up with a big tax bill. So, if you decide to go down the SMSF path, do your due diligence, engage professionals and seek advice.

How much do you need to save in super for retirement?

The million-dollar retirement goal gets a lot of attention. But, is it the right number? A better question is: for you, how much is enough?

Carol, age 65, draws her 5% minimum pension of $50,000 a year from her $1 million super nest egg. She doesn't need to dip into her retirement capital; it's just a bonus.

Rob and Alex want to enjoy a more luxurious life, including overseas travel and paying for their grandchildren's education. They'll need $3 million or $4 million.

A million dollars, then, may be enough for some but not for others.

We find that a useful benchmark is the Association of Superannuation Funds (ASFA) Retirement Standard. The data (June quarter 2020) indicates that a couple aged around 65 who own their home and enjoy a comfortable lifestyle spend around $62,000 a year while a single person needs around $44,000. For a modest lifestyle, a couple needs around $40,000 a year and a single person around $28,000.

ASFA has also estimated the savings people may need at retirement – they assume that the individuals will spend all their capital, and receive a part Age Pension. In this case, a couple seeking a comfortable lifestyle would need $640,000 saved, and a single person $545,000.

For someone seeking a modest lifestyle, because they are likely to receive a full Age Pension, ASFA estimates that they only need $70,000 (single or couple) as their nest egg.

HOW AM I TRACKING?

To work out how you're tracking and how much you might need when you retire, try the helpful calculators on the Super Guru site: www.superguru.com.au/calculators

At the end of the day, remember money is personal. There's no magic number except the one enabling you to live the life you've dreamed.

 QUICK STEPS

- Calculate how much you might need in retirement – and how you're tracking: http://www.superguru.com.au/calculators

- Compare your current super – use the ChantWest "Apple Check". Are you paying too much? Should you change or combine funds?

- Review how your money is invested. Go back to our section on investments and check you are comfortable with the level of risk.

- Boost your super – make extra before- and after-tax contributions.

- Check if you or your partner can benefit from any bonuses, like the spouse super offset, the co-contribution, or the low income super tax offset.

- If you're not sure what to do, seek advice. Super is complex and even a little advice can go a long way.

5

INSURANCE

THE BEST RESULT FROM YOUR INSURANCE IS TO FIND YOU NEVER NEED TO CLAIM – BUT IF YOU DO, THE WORST THING IS NOT HAVING THE RIGHT INSURANCE IN PLACE

 LIVING ON A PRAYER

By now, you probably realise that real life is unpredictable. Unlike the movies, few things turn out quite as we planned – for better or worse.

And particularly for those things that go into the "worse" camp, this unpredictability is why it's so important to make sure that you have a safety net. Few of us can prevent bad things from happening. Most of us can make sure that we have enough money to support us when they do.

And that's where life insurance comes in.

But isn't insurance a waste of money?

Okay, so before we get into what type of insurance and how much, if you're like some people, you're wondering if insurance isn't just a waste of money. Particularly as you get into your 40s and older when the premiums often begin to ratchet up.

Here's the secret about insurance: you should never want to need to use it. Nobody ever said "great, I've been diagnosed with cancer, now I can put my insurance to good use".

You don't buy insurance because you want it to pay out. You buy it in case you need it to. You buy it so that you have the peace of mind that if something bad happens to you – or someone in your world – you will be financially taken care of.

If you spend tens of thousands of dollars on insurance and come out with nothing, you're a winner.

To illustrate this, we love this chart created by Colin Lalley in his blog: "Insurance genius: why life insurance isn't a gamble, even if it never pays out":

1. Very lucky duck
This is the fairy tale scenario. You don't pay for insurance, and you're very lucky as you never need it.

2. Lucky duck

This is a positive scenario. You buy insurance and you're lucky enough to never use it. You enjoy life not having to worry about the financial impact of something bad happen – and have the good fortune that nothing does. You out-live and out-health your insurance cover.

3. Close call duck

This too is a positive scenario. You buy insurance – which is lucky – because you do need to use it. You are ill or injured – or you die – and you and your family have the security of a financial safety net.

4. Dead duck

This is the worst case scenario. You bet on not buying insurance. You are ill or injured or you die. You and/or your family are under financial strain. No one is happy with this outcome.

You don't have control over what bad things may happen to you. You do have control over how you mitigate the financial impact of those risks.

	NOTHING BAD HAPPENS	SOMETHING BAD HAPPENS
NOT INSURED	1. VERY LUCKY DUCK	4. DEAD DUCK
INSURED	2. LUCKY DUCK	3. CLOSE CALL DUCK

So, what types of risks, you might ask.

Just living our everyday lives, we face innumerable risks. And it would be impossible to protect ourselves against every one of them.

It makes sense to focus on the main risks – and we suggest that you think carefully about two things:

• How likely is it that a particular "bump in the road" might happen?
• And if it did, would it overwhelm you financially?

Here are the main "bumps in the road" that could disrupt your lifestyle – and your family's world – along with an indication of how likely they are to occur (based on claims paid by the insurers), the money matters you may want to consider, and the type of insurance that can help:

EVENT Dying
TYPE OF INSURANCE Life insurance
PROPORTION OF CLAIMS 33%
MONEY MATTERS If you have family and dependents, you want to make sure that they have enough money to live their lives without being stressed-out financially.

Most people like to repay at least some of the mortgage, cover the kids' education and ensure that there's enough ongoing income to help pay day-to-day expenses.

Many like to make sure that their spouse has a buffer so that they can take a break from work to grieve and adjust.

Some people like to set aside some money for the causes they support.

EVENT Serious and prolonged illness or injury that prevents you from working for a time
TYPE OF INSURANCE Income protection
PROPORTION OF CLAIMS 33%
MONEY MATTERS If you are working and earning an income then it's highly likely that you need income protection insurance. This is designed to replace most of your income in the event that you can't work for an extended period – maybe months or even years.

Income protection typically replaces most – 75% of your earned income – so that you can meet your day-to-day living expenses.

Some policies will enable you to elect an additional 10% which tops up your super.

It doesn't matter if you have financial dependents, or if you own a home, this is your most essential insurance – anyone who relies on their work income to pay their expenses needs income protection.

EVENT Critical illness that involves serious medical intervention
TYPE OF INSURANCE Critical illness or trauma
PROPORTION OF CLAIMS 23%
MONEY MATTERS If you're unlucky enough to get knocked for six by a critical illness or trauma – like cancer, heart attack or a stroke – then you will most likely need significant medical treatment.
This can be very expensive.
Which is where critical illness insurance comes in. It is designed to provide you with a lump sum to help you pay for your expenses. And interestingly, they don't even have to be medical expenses – you can pay for transport to get to and from hospital, for extra care or help around the house, or even a holiday to help you rest and recover.

EVENT Serious and prolonged illness or injury that prevents you from working ever again
TYPE OF INSURANCE Total & permanent disability
PROPORTION OF CLAIMS 10%
MONEY MATTERS If you are permanently prevented by illness or injury from working – and so can't earn an income – this is where Total & Permanent Disability (TPD) kicks in.
While income protection provides some income replacement for a temporary disability, TPD insurance offers a lump sum payment to help you repay debt and meet living and additional care expenses.
If you have income protection, then this can help reduce the amount of TPD cover you may need.
Again with TPD, it doesn't matter if you have financial dependents, or if you own a home, this is an important insurance to ensure that you have the best chance of being looked after financially over your lifetime.

Source: www.insurancewatch.com.au/insurance-claims-statistics.html

Child trauma cover

We've talked here about your own critical illness or trauma, but sometimes it is the critical illness endured by a young child that is the most challenging, emotionally and financially. If a child is critically ill, none of your other insurances kick in. If you need to take time off work to care for a seriously ill child, you are not able to claim on your income protection – which only applies if you are seriously ill or injured. You can't claim on your own critical illness either.

We are fans of child trauma cover for children aged 2 up to 16. While you hope you never have to claim on it, it is reasonably priced and, in the event of a child being critically ill, worth every single cent.

How much do you need?

Here are the questions to ask yourself to help identify your insurance needs. We've also included a few case studies to give you an idea of how to put the pieces of the insurance puzzle together.

We call this our BLISS framework:

BLISS framework

Bumps that could disrupt your lifestyle?

Liabilities that you need to pay (current like mortgage, or future like kids' education)?

Income you need to replace?

Savings you can draw on?

Safety net of existing insurance?

What are the bumps that could disrupt your lifestyle?

The most common ones where life insurance can help are:

- You (or your spouse/partner) die.
- You (or your spouse/partner) become so ill or injured that you can't ever work again.
- You (or your spouse/partner) become seriously ill and can't work.
- You (or your spouse/partner) suffers a critical illness and need significant medical treatment.
- Your child suffers a critical illness and needs significant medical aid.

There are of course other bumps that have a financial impact. For instance, we're often asked if there is insurance for losing your job. There's not – and if there was the likelihood of it occurring would make the risk so high that the cost would be untenable for most people. And then of course, there are other things which involve the things you own – like your car or your house – which you should consider insuring. These are generally pretty straightforward – and so we're going to stay focused on the life matters here.

What liabilities do you need – or want – to repay in the event of a "bump"?

If you have no loans, then skip to the "income" section. If you do have loans, then ask yourself these questions:

- Would you want to make any loan repayments – in part or in full?
- If you have a spouse/partner, what loan amount could they comfortably service? Would you want them to be debt-free so that they don't have to worry about a loan at all? Or would you want to reduce the loan to a more manageable level?
- What amount would you wish to repay in the event of your:
  a. Death?
  b. Permanent disability?
  c. Temporary disability?
  d. Critical illness?

What income would you need to replace?

- How much money each year would you need to maintain your lifestyle?

- How much money each year would your spouse/partner need to help meet expenses?

- Would you want to have any additional money each year for medical expenses and care?

- What is the amount of any other income you (or your family) would receive that might offset your income needs? For example, annual or long service leave; or in the event of permanent disability you may receive income protection benefits for a period.

- What would the annual amount be in the event of your: Death? Permanent disability? Temporary disability? Critical illness?

What savings can you draw on?

- What assets could be sold to put towards repaying any loans or expenses? This may include money held in your emergency cash buffer, in an investment account, or (if you're able to access it) your super.

- What would the amount of savings you could use in the event of your: Death? Permanent disability? Temporary disability? Critical illness?

What safety net of existing insurance can you claim on?

- What insurances do you have on which you could claim? Maybe you have Life & TPD in your super. If you have income protection insurance, then this can help to offset the amount of TPD or Critical Illness cover you may need.

- What insurances might you be able to claim on in the event of your: Death? Permanent disability? Temporary disability? Critical illness?

Once you've worked through these questions – and if you have a spouse/ partner discussed what you both need to have in place – then it's a good idea to try some of the online insurance calculators as these make it easy to get an idea of how much you may need.

www.lifewise.org.au/

www.moneysmart.gov.au/tools-and-resources/calculators-and-apps/ life-insurance-calculator

WHAT ABOUT ME?

When you're thinking about insurance, it's important to remember, it's not just about you.

It's also valuable to think about who in your world – if something happened to them and they didn't have insurance, or enough of it – would be relying on you.

Maybe it's your young adult children, who happily moved out to be independent. And here they are with a serious illness, not able to work, and no insurance to pay their rent or living costs. Back at home and eating into your retirement savings.

Maybe it's your children who have kids. Or the parents of your godchildren.

Talk to them about getting their insurances sorted so that their lack of planning doesn't impact your financial security and freedom.

CASE STUDIES

Janine aged 34 is enjoying single life. A solicitor with a leading firm, she earns $90,000 a year, has no debts and has just started investing $1,000 a month. She is not planning to settle down just yet – and is pursuing her career including looking at new opportunities to build her skills.

What are her insurance protection priorities?

Income protection and most likely with a benefit period to age 65 – which would give Janine income replacement over the long term. As Janine has good cashflow – and she is looking to potentially move employers – it may make sense to hold her income protection personally rather than through super as this will give Janine more choices about how she structures her cover, and make it easier to keep the cover constant even with job changes.

Ranier is 45, married to Simon 43, and together they have three children aged 12, 9 and 6. They each earn incomes of $90,000 and their annual expenses are $150,000 including mortgage repayments. While the kids attend the local high school, Ranier and Simon prioritise education and have private tutors to help the kids. They have a mortgage of $750,000.

What are their insurance protection priorities?

Income protection is a must. In addition, Ranier and Simon both need life insurance and TPD insurance so that they could repay their mortgage, and ensure that they have enough money to meet the family's living expenses. If either one of them was to die or become permanently disabled, the other wouldn't otherwise have enough income to keep up mortgage repayments and fund the family's expenses.

It would also make sense for them to consider Critical Illness cover to give them a buffer if either were to suffer a traumatic illness. And, of course, Child Trauma cover could be a valuable addition to their family's protection.

Michaela is age 55, divorced with two adult children who are on their own two feet and earning good incomes. She runs her own business and earns $100,000 a year. She owns her home with a remaining mortgage of $200,000 and cash in her offset account of $100,000 which she keeps for a rainy day. She is working hard to boost her super and has a balance of $600,000.

What are her insurance protection priorities?

Income protection which would help her to meet her living expenses and keep topping up her super. In this case, as her income may vary as a business owner, it could be helpful to have an 'agreed value' income protection policy.

TPD insurance to cover her mortgage and potentially provide a top up to her super as well. She may want to consider Critical Illness cover – again to ensure that she doesn't need to redraw on her mortgage or dip into her savings.

And almost as importantly, Michaela should ensure that her adult children have income protection insurance as a baseline. Why? Because if anything were to happen to them and they could not work for a period, guess where they may end up... back relying on Michaela. If she had to support an adult child, it could easily undo all the hard savings work she has been doing.

THE FINE PRINT

Waiting period: Typically for income protection, this is the period of time (often 30 to 90 days) before you can make a claim.

Benefit period: Again, for income protection, this is how long you can expect to receive benefits – usually two years, five years or to age 65.

Own occupation vs any occupation Total & Permanent Disability (TPD): This occupation definition is important as it can influence how easy (or hard) it is for you to be able to successfully claim on your TPD policy. An "own" occupation definition gives you a better opportunity to make a successful claim – as the criteria is based on you not being able to perform your own occupation. It does cost a little more. The alternative is an "any" occupation definition. This is the type of policy which can be owned within a superannuation fund. However, the bar you need to reach in terms of disability is higher. To successfully claim you would need to be assessed as unable to do any occupation reasonably suited to you by education, training and experience.

Agreed value vs indemnity: This option relates to income protection and when the insurer calculates the amount of your benefit. With "agreed value", as the name suggests, the amount of your benefit is agreed upfront. You provide evidence of your income at the time you apply for the policy, and the insurer agrees to cover you for a fixed benefit based on that income, regardless of any subsequent change in income. It does cost a little more in premiums – but it can be worth it for the certainty of outcome, particularly handy for anyone likely to have future changes. in their income. On the other hand, with an "indemnity" policy, your benefit is calculated when you submit your claim. This will either be the dollar amount you are insured for, or a given percentage of your actual pre-disability income, whichever is lower. The challenge here is, if your income has reduced since taking out the cover, you may find that you have been paying premiums for a benefit amount that you are not eligible to receive. Ouch.

Tax deductibility: If you own your income protection policy personally, premiums are generally tax deductible (life, TPD and Trauma premiums are not). If you own Life, TPD (any occupation) or Income Protection in super (trauma can't be held in super), then the super fund may be able to claim a tax deduction for premiums paid. However, in the event of a successful claim for TPD in super or income protection, beware that tax is applied to the monies paid out.

Standard vs luxury cover: Just like with cars, you can opt for the standard version of insurance or the "luxury" version which comes with additional features at an extra cost. Always check the list of features to ensure that they add value to you before signing for the top level of cover.

Loadings and exclusions: When you apply for insurance cover, you need to answer a range of questions – including some regarding your personal medical history, family medical history and your pastimes. Your answers to the questions may mean that you have increased risk factors under the policy. Your cover may have a premium loading – which means that you pay a higher premium for the cover. In some cases, you may not be offered cover. In others, you may not be covered if you suffer a specified excluded medical condition, or you are injured or die as a result of participating in an excluded pastime or activity.

Stepped vs level premiums: These are two different types of premium (cost) structures. Stepped premiums are re-calculated each year based on age, and generally means your costs are lower in early years compared to level premiums, but become more expensive as you get older – and have increasing risks. Level premiums mean the cost of your insurance cover doesn't increase due to your age (though the cover and the premium may go up with expenses and inflation). Level premiums can give you more certainty on cost when planning ahead for the future and can be helpful if you're planning to keep your insurance cover for many years.

Future life events (to increase your cover): Future life events means you can increase your Life Insurance, TPD, Critical Illness or income protection policy amounts without evidence of your health or pastimes. For example, getting married or divorced, obtaining or increasing a mortgage, getting a pay rise or increasing your financial stake in a business. Take note: policies may have an age limit on this – like age 55.

INSURANCE WITHIN SUPER OR OUTSIDE?

You can hold three of the four main types of personal insurance through super: life, total and permanent disability (TPD) and income protection. Critical Illness cover (including child trauma) can't be held within super.

Here is a summary of some of the pros and cons of holding your insurance through super.

Advantages

- No drain on cashflow: Premiums are deducted from your superannuation account balance rather than out of your personal funds which can help your day-to-day cash flow.

- Premiums may be lower: Because super funds may be able to negotiate a better rate your cover within super may be cheaper than the same amount of insurance outside super. Be aware, however, that you may trade-off other factors like tax, additional features, certainty of a potential payout and the time taken to receive a payment.

- You may not need to do medical tests: If you are applying for a cover amount that is within your super fund's automatic acceptance limit (AAL), you may not need to do any medical tests. However, if you want to apply for a higher level of cover then medical tests may apply.

- If you salary sacrifice to fund your premiums, the premium is essentially tax deductible. This not only helps to reduce the drain on your super account, it also can be tax-effective where your income tax rate is higher than the super contribution tax rate.

Disadvantages

- Insurance premiums will reduce your super savings: If you pay premiums from your super balance, then you will have less money in your account to grow over time. This is the dark side of compounding – as the cost of these premiums create a drag on the benefits of compounding of investment returns.

- Tax payable on death benefits: If death benefits are paid to a beneficiary who is not financially dependent on you – like an adult child – they may be taxed on the proceeds.

- Tax on TPD benefits: If you withdraw a TPD benefit from superannuation prior to your preservation age (which is between ages 55 and 60 depending on your date of birth – see the super section for more details) you need to be aware that tax is payable on the benefit.

- Benefit payments can be delayed: If you are successful in making a claim on your insurance, your payment has to do a two-step process. It is first paid from the insurer to your superannuation fund; and then if the Trustee of the super fund approves the payment, from the super fund to you. This can cause delays in the payment to you, particularly for death and TPD benefits.

- It's not easy to transfer your cover if you change super funds: If you change super funds, you may not be able to transfer your insurance. This could restrict your flexibility in combining or moving super funds as you may need to apply for new insurance.

- Limited choice in how you structure your insurance cover: For example, within super, most funds only offer "stepped" premium policies. With income protection you may not have your preferred choice of waiting period or benefit period. And with TPD, you can't hold an "own" occupation through super (though some super funds now offer a super-linked option which can be worth exploring).

- Critical illness (trauma) insurance is not available through super: Because this type of insurance doesn't fit within the purpose of super, it has to be held outside your super fund.

- You may not be able to guarantee who the beneficiary will be: Some super funds don't allow you to determine who you want to receive your benefits upon your death – this is known as a non-binding death benefit nomination. If you need absolute certainty of who will receive the death benefit, super fund insurance cover may not be for you.

When you may not need personal insurance

Simple economics says you shouldn't pay for something you don't need. It doesn't matter if you're talking about a purple pair of shoes, Netflix or personal insurance.

Life insurance If you don't have a partner or spouse, or financially dependent kids, then you may not need life insurance. If your mortgage is paid off, your kids are through uni, you have an emergency fund and enough for retirement, life insurance may be an unnecessary expense.

Income protection insurance If you have enough money in savings to meet your lifestyle expenses without needing to work, then you probably don't need income protection insurance.

Critical illness insurance If you have enough money in savings to spend say $100,000 to $200,000 on medical and recovery expenses – and still be on track for retirement, you may not need critical illness insurance.

MENTAL ILLNESS AND LIFE INSURANCE

Mental illness is a sensitive and important topic. Even more so when it comes to applying for life insurance – particularly disability insurance.

Mental health conditions are in the top three reasons for disability claims in Australia and the incidence of claims is increasing. Because of this, insurance companies are often selective when assessing disability insurance applications. If you've experienced a mental illness, whether or not that condition was disabling, insurance companies will consider you to be statistically more likely to make a claim in the future. This can affect the terms under which an insurer may be prepared to offer you life insurance. Each insurance company offers different products and assessments so if you're concerned about a mental health condition and obtaining insurance, you should make sure you understand the application options and process. For example, online applications may have different underwriting guidelines to other products regarding past and present illnesses. We strongly recommend that before making any decision, you speak first to the insurance company. You should also read and understand the Product Disclosure Statement (PDS) as it fully describes the product, benefits and limitations. This is definitely a situation where it's worth speaking with a financial adviser or insurance broker qualified to advise which products are likely to be best for you.

6 Top Tips

1. Design your life insurance plan as part of your overall plan. That plan should take into account future expenses, such as education costs, and the future growth of your income or assets.

2. Don't skimp. Buy a little more cover than you'll need to give you a buffer. It often gets harder to increase your insurance as you age.

3. Calculate the impact of taxes. Total & Permanent Disability payouts from super may be subject to tax when the payment is made. Income protection benefits are taxed as income.

4. Structure your policies into separate jigsaw pieces to give you the flexibility to vary your cover as your needs ebb and flow. This can also help reduce your lifetime cost of cover.

5. Read the fine print. Make sure you know exactly what is and isn't covered. Give yourself the very best chance of being able to claim.

6. Review your insurance cover each year. Your world will change. You may need more of one type of insurance and less of another, or even less of all your insurances. Don't pay for insurance you no longer need.

✈ QUICK STEPS

- Try one of the online insurance calculators to help you work out how much and what type of insurance you might need. Think about what things you wish to insure for, and the amount you'd like to cover.

- At minimum, if you're earning an income and reliant on that income, it's likely you'll need income protection. If you don't have time to shop around, at least get cover through your super fund.

- If you have a home loan, then a reasonable rule of thumb is to have enough Life cover and enough TPD insurance to pay out the loan.

- Don't risk others in your world having an illness, injury or dying and disrupting your plans. Make sure they get their insurances sorted too.

- Insurance can be complex. Seek professional advice.

ILLNESS / DISABILITY

We can make our plans, but the Lord determines our steps: Psalms 21.

Or as Woody Allen translates it "If you want to make God laugh, tell him about your plans."

145,000

new cases of cancer are estimated to be diagnosed in 2018

90.1%

is the five-year survival rate for breast cancer

61.1 YEARS

is the median age of breast cancer diagnosis

Cancer is **NOT THE ONLY MAJOR ILLNESS** to strike people in their prime.

(Cancer Council 2019)

This should not deter us from making plans, but our plans have to include some sort of allowance for things to go wrong – breast cancer, other cancers, MS, heart disease happen.

According to a Deloitte Economics Report commissioned by the Breast Cancer Network of Australia, released in 2018, out-of-pocket costs can reach into the tens of thousands of dollars and add considerably to the stress of cancer. The highest proportion of respondents to the survey were in the 50–59-year-old age group.

Breast cancer pushes many women, and their families, to the financial brink, where they are reliant on financial assistance from family, friends and their communities. Women with private health insurance typically pay around double the out-of-pocket costs of those who do not hold private health insurance.

The research found funding the cost of treatment and care for early breast cancer can stretch people's budgets to breaking point. Australia's health care system through Medicare covers about half of all services. However, most people (88%) will have some out-of-pocket cost for their treatment and care. Breast reconstruction surgery, radiotherapy treatment, breast MRI scans, genomic tests such as Oncotype DX, and genetic testing are some of the biggest expenses.

The cost for a woman who has private health insurance is typically around $7,000, but can be more than $21,000. The cost for a woman without private health insurance is usually around $3,600. Overall, the typical cost for all respondents with early breast cancer was around $5,000 over the five-year period for which this survey collected data, with the majority of those costs incurred within the first two years from diagnosis.

This is compounded by the cost of lost paid work hours and super contributions during this time. Partners may also reduce work hours to attend appointments and provide care. The survey found that the total number of household hours worked dropped by 50 per cent in the first year after a breast cancer diagnosis.

Around two thirds of women (67%) paid for their breast cancer treatment by using household savings. Many used their "nest egg" – money that was being saved for something particular such as a house deposit, retirement, travel or another significant goal – to support themselves and their families during treatment. Using this money to fund cancer treatment changes people's plans with years of careful saving lost.

Somewhat alarmingly, the financial losses cannot be made up easily and sometimes not at all. They are likely to affect most cancer sufferers or those with other chronic conditions such as MS.

A very fit female friend in her early 40s was rushed to hospital a year ago as she found her breathing to be difficult and tests showed a blockage to her heart. She needed a triple bypass and had the option, through having a good trauma policy (recommended by a financial adviser) to choose a robotic keyhole surgery (which was less invasive, had shorter recovery period and smaller scarring). Without the insurance cover she would not have been able to afford this.

Another friend, who was diagnosed with MS in her late-30s has had her work life curtailed, her medical expenses skyrocket and needs to fundraise for money for further treatment. This not only impacts her own finances now and for the future but her father has cashed in some of his super and her mother had to stop her paid work to take care of her.

We can't stop living to make sure we always have enough money to see us through a major setback but we can look at ways to cover the financial risk and help us through serious health crises.

6

BORROWING MONEY

THERE ARE GOOD REASONS TO BORROW MONEY AND THERE ARE BAD – BUT WHATEVER YOUR REASONS YOU NEED TO KNOW THE BEST WAY OF USING SOMEONE ELSE'S MONEY

I NEED YOU TONIGHT

For most people debt or borrowed money is a necessary evil. But debt can help us set ourselves up financially. So it's worth spending a moment to talk about why debt is helpful, and then to assess the pros and cons of borrowing.

The first question to ask is: why are you borrowing money?

In most cases, it will be to help you overcome a timing difference – that is, you can bring forward a purchase or investment to the present, with the intention of repaying the money in future when you have more income and assets.

Student loan debt is a good example of timing mismatch. Once you have your qualifications, you can most likely command a higher salary than before you earn your education but you have to pay for your education first. So being able to borrow money to pay your upfront education costs and then paying the money back later out of your expected higher earnings is a valuable way to pay for the costs. So that's an example of where debt would probably be considered good.

There are also situations where it's not desirable. So let's talk about the different types of debt.

BORROWING TO INVEST

Some people borrow money to invest. This may be for an investment property, to buy shares or create an investment portfolio, or perhaps to build a business.

One of the attractions is the potential to claim the interest on your loan as a tax deduction – that is, unlike a home loan, the debt is likely to be tax deductible.

This is also known as "gearing". You might negatively gear – in which case your income is less than the cost of your interest and other investment expenses. Or you might positively gear – where your income is more than your expenses and you're making a profit. Or you may be neutrally geared where your income matches your expenses.

Now many people get very excited about negative gearing. But they often forget one key thing. And that is: the first rule of investing is to profit from the investment; investing decisions should not be driven by tax.

They also forget that, whatever type of gearing is used, it is still costing you money.

NEGATIVE GEARING

Let's take a closer look at negative gearing and how it really works.

In this case your investment is making a loss. The income – whether rent or dividends – is less than the interest and expenses of having the investment. You can apply that loss against your overall income – so that when it comes to tax time, your assessable income is lower and you should pay less tax.

For example, let's say you are on a 45% marginal tax rate (excluding the medicare levy). Your expenses are $10,000. And so, when you put in your tax return, you receive $4,500 back. That means you are $5,500 worse off thanks to your investment.

Now imagine you're on the 19 per cent tax bracket. Your tax saving would be smaller ($1,900) and your loss would be bigger ($8,100).

So why would anyone use negative gearing? They are pinning their hopes on the expectation that the investment will grow in value. The trick is, they need gains that are greater than their annual losses. And that's after accounting for capital gains tax.

There's no guarantee that your investment can achieve that. In fact, you need to consider what happens if your investment were to go backwards. Gearing is a risky strategy.

The question we always ask is: what could you have earned by simply investing in a well-diversified portfolio? Or even putting your money in a very secure term deposit?

PREPAYMENT OF DEDUCTIBLE INTEREST

Prepaying interest on an investment loan is a way of bringing forward a tax saving that would have been claimed the next financial year. This may be helpful if you want to gain an early tax benefit. It can also be valuable if you have an unusually high taxable income in a given financial year.

However, there are some downsides:

- You need to have the cash to make the interest prepayment.
- You are locking in a payment – if you were to sell the asset in the following year, you may need to break your fixed term payment which is likely to incur penalties.
- You are locking in an interest rate – of course, if interest rates rise, you may be better off; however, if they fall, then you would be paying a higher rate of interest than the going market rate.
- If you go back to paying interest monthly or fortnightly, then there will be a year where you won't have any interest deduction.

HOME LOANS

One of the most common types of borrowing is taking out a loan to buy a house. When interest rates are very low – as they are now – a home loan can be a very useful strategy.

Some people may even be better off not using surplus cashflow to pay debt faster – and instead could use that cashflow to boost savings, especially super.

In other words, if you owe $100,000 on your house at 3.75% interest, you're paying interest at the rate of $3,750 per year.

However, if you can invest that and earn, say a 6% return, you'll make $6,000 in a year. Allowing for superannuation income tax of 15% ($900), that's $5,100 and still $1,350 more than the cost of interest on your home loan.

LIFESTYLE LOANS

We are not fans of lifestyle loans – things like using a credit card to purchase your new season wardrobe or taking out a personal loan to buy a car.

Why? First, the item you're purchasing is unlikely to grow your wealth – in fact, it's probably going to drain it. And second, the loan will be unsecured and so cost you a bomb.

Here are some examples:

- **Credit cards** Did you know that typical interest rates for credit cards range from 10% to 30%? If you rack up expenses on your credit card and can't repay the balance each month, then you're building a mountain of very expensive debt. The cost of the interest alone creates a higher risk that you don't repay the balance and your debt snowballs.

- **Car loans** You may need a car – but if you don't have enough savings to buy one, then taking out a loan is a very expensive exercise. Even more so if you buy a new car, as it loses value (depreciates) as soon as you drive it out of the car yard. Paying interest for years on an asset that is losing value is not a smart move.

- **Buy-now-pay later** While these schemes may look like a "free lunch", beware the traps. First, it can give you a false sense of affordability (see box p118). Second, if you miss a payment you may rack up unexpected fees and charges (one provider makes 25% of its revenues from consumer late payment fees). And third, if you link your account to a credit card and your repayments get away from you, you'll be paying super-expensive interest.

PROFILE

NAME
REGINA

AGE 56

INCOME BRACKET
>$180,000

RELATIONSHIP SITUATION
MARRIED

SUPER BALANCE
$400,000

FINANCIAL ADVISER
NO

OTHER INVESTMENTS

Apartment in Canberra, bought 7 years ago, through Defence Housing Australia worth about $500,000 (interest only loan).

ESTIMATED ANNUAL SAVINGS

We probably managed to jointly save $20,000 a year which we put into house, savings account, super.

DESIRED AGE OF RETIREMENT

Not sure ever want to retire but definitely don't want to work the same as now, possibly work part-time, contract, something different. And maybe in a different field.

DESIRED RETIREMENT LIFESTYLE WISE

Overseas travel constantly – five or six times a year. Continue the same lifestyle and not struggling for money if I want to buy a new dress, handbag, or gift.

WHERE YOU ARE CURRENTLY

Working full time in financial services, travelling once or twice a year overseas, going to the theatre regularly, eating out often. We don't splurge too much on those things but we are able to do them in a more than comfortable way. We have been able in the last few years to do more because school fees ended a few years ago. My husband is working full time and we are both intending to work like this until aged 60, then will look at other options.

WHAT YOU'D LIKE TO BE DOING IN THE FUTURE

Part-time work, enjoying life: travelling, being financially comfortable. We have one daughter and will likely pay for her wedding, and cover her HECS fees.

I want to stay in Sydney in our apartment. It suits us perfectly. It's close to amenities, family, and the lifestyle we enjoy. I also want to ensure we remain close to healthcare facilities – I wouldn't want to move somewhere without hospitals or specialists.

HOW YOU'RE PLANNING ON REACHING THERE

My plan right now is to put any savings and excess cash into super. We don't have a big home loan now and while we can put a bit into the home loan we've started really focusing on our super. Also, we're both likely to receive some sort of benefits from parents but then we're probably going to use some of this to help our daughter enter the property market.

CURRENT PRIORITIES

Put as much into super as possible. We have a holiday to America in August which is paid for and we will plan a holiday next year. I also want a new kitchen and I'll have to pay for that. We will save first as we don't like to take on extra debt. And you never know what's around the corner; we had a levy on our unit this year $17,000 so you need to keep money aside.

FINANCIAL DECISIONS THAT HELPED YOU

We've always fully paid our credit cards each month, and when we sold our house to buy this apartment we had a much smaller mortgage which we should pay off in the next five years. We are also thinking if/when we sell our Canberra property it would pay off the mortgage. We are currently paying it as an interest only loan and we'd consider whether selling it would pay the debt. Meanwhile the rent is almost covering the full cost of the property.

FINANCIAL SITUATIONS THAT AFFECTED YOUR GOALS TO DATE

A redundancy payment a few years ago helped reduce the mortgage.

School fees have been paid for one daughter.

We bought an investment property

20 years ago but were burned when we had tenants who ruined the property and we had to sell at a loss. Our defence investment prevents you having to face that because it goes to defence personnel and you never have to worry about finding tenants. I asked financial advisers about it, and they said you pay more in fees but I think it's worth it to ensure that you always have people renting it who will take care of it. The idea is you hold it for 7 years then sell or keep. However, it can't be sold to just anyone.

OTHER COMMENTS

I wish I'd focused on this earlier. I wish I had known more about super, it's a great investment vehicle. If I'd been salary sacrificing that would have been incredible. I had funds everywhere, I hadn't put in extra. Now I focus on super and add more when I can.

My plan right now is to put any savings and excess cash into super

The real cost of debt

The primary cost of debt is the interest that you need to pay – it's the price you pay to use someone else's money to buy something now that you otherwise don't have the money to afford.

But most people don't appreciate just how expensive debt can be.

Here's what the real cost of a $10,000 loan is over 5-year and 10-year periods with the typical range of rates of interest for credit cards and personal loans:

	5 YEARS	10 YEARS
10%	$12,748	$15,858
15%	$14,274	$19,360
20%	$15,896	$23,191

Looking at it another way: for every dollar, at 10% p.a. interest over five years you pay $1.27. And at a 20% p.a. interest rate over 10 years, for every dollar you're really spending almost $2.32.

If you're interested to check out the real cost of your debt, try this useful calculator:

www.moneysmart.gov.au/tools-and-resources/calculators-and-apps/ personal-loan-calculator

CASE STUDY

Elle decided to buy a new car. She paid $15,000 using $5,000 from her savings, with $10,000 funded through a five-year personal loan from her bank. When Kate checked the interest rate on her loan, she found that Elle's personal loan had an interest rate of 15%. Elle was coughing up $238 a month in repayments – with her total interest bill over the five-year loan period a whopping $4,274.

So, the real cost of Elle's car is not $15,000. It's $19,274 – almost 33% more.

The extra cost of missed opportunity

The other key factor in the real cost of debt is the extra cost of missed opportunity – that is, what else could you have done with the money that you've been using to repay debt.

Let's imagine that Elle decided that she could do without a car. She now has zero debt and $5,000 as a starting investment. Let's say that she now invests $238 a month (the same amount that she was using to fund repayments). After five years, if her investment returned 6% a year, she would have $23,350.

The interest on the debt cost Elle $4,274. But the overall decision cost her an estimated $23,350 in lost opportunity.

Initial deposit **$5,000**
Regular Deposits **$14,280**
Total interest **$4,070**

Total Savings
$23,350

TIPS TO BE DEBT-FREE

You'll hear many tips on how to become debt free.

One is the snowball, where you pay the smallest value debt first regardless of the rate of interest. The idea is that you gain a psychological win by knocking off one debt.

We prefer a financial-first approach – which means doing everything you can to reduce debt with the highest interest rate first:

1. Write a list of any debts including the amount and the interest rate.

2. Find out if you can transfer the debt to a lower interest rate – maybe even zero. You may be able to consolidate your credit card debt into a zero rate credit card for a period of time. If you have a mortgage with room in your credit limit, then you're likely to be better off re-drawing on your mortgage to repay higher interest rate debt.

3. Investigate the "family bank". Maybe your parents have savings that they could loan you at a rate of interest that suits you both – higher than what they may be able to earn in a cash account and lower than what you're paying on your credit card or personal loan. Even if they have a mortgage, they may be able to offer you their mortgage interest rate which is likely to be much less than a credit card or personal loan.

4. Direct every cent of savings and surplus cashflow into your remaining highest interest rate debt first. You may want to create additional savings by selling things you don't really need.

5. Celebrate your wins in a way that's no-spend.

Don't even consider paying extra on your home loan or student loan if you have credit card or other high-interest debt.

HOME LOAN OFFSET ACCOUNTS

Parking your savings in a home loan offset account can be a good way to cut your home loan interest while keeping the flexibility to draw on your money if you need to.

An offset account is a bank account linked to your home loan. The money you have in that account offsets the balance of your loan – reducing the amount of interest you pay every month. This can help you to pay your loan off faster.

We recommend looking for a bank which offers the option to have multiple offset cash accounts linked to one home loan, which can help to have all of your cash accounts (day-to-day, emergency and fun accounts) working to offset the balance of your loan.

Here's how it works

Let's say you have a home loan of $500,000 with an annual interest rate of 4%, and $100,000 in your cash offset account. You'll only pay interest on $400,000. Over the life of a 30-year loan, you can save more than $171,870. If you need to use your $100,000 in your cash offset for an emergency, you can.

And because the money in the cash account effectively reduces the value of your home loan for the purposes of calculating interest, there is no interest income to add to your income tax assessment.

What's the downside?

- Home loans with an offset account may have a higher interest rate than a loan without an offset.
- Some loan providers only allow a partial offset.
- Some home loans have a monthly account keeping fee and some have withdrawal fees.

INTEREST-ONLY HOME LOANS

It seems that many people are tempted by home loans that are interest-only – mainly because, compared with a traditional loan, the regular repayments are lower. Most home loans are "principal and interest", which means your regular payments cover your interest costs and a repayment of the loan balance – so over time, you eliminate your debt.

Interest only loans work differently – you only pay the interest and your loan balance stays the same. This could be a good strategy in certain circumstances. For example, it may make sense if you have irregular income – like variable cashflow from a business or commissions. It can lower your monthly mortgage costs and you maybe able to pay more when you have extra money. It may also be a short-term strategy, if you are taking a break from work.

However, over the long term an interest-only loan can cause trouble.

- The interest-only period is usually for a set timeframe (say, five years) after which the loan changes to a principal and interest. Unless you can secure an additional interest-only term, you will need to repay both principal and interest – which could increase your repayments.
- It will cost you more. For example, a $500,000 loan over 25 years, with an annual interest rate of 5%, would cost you approximately $40,000 more in interest if it was interest-only for the first five years.
- You're not increasing equity. If your property does not increase in value during the interest-only period, you risk having no extra equity in your home at the end of this period, despite making payments every month. This creates risk if house prices drop or you need to sell.

BORROWING MONEY IS NEVER RISK FREE

Regardless of the type of borrowing, it's never risk free. And the more you borrow the greater the risk.

- Interest rates could rise. If they rose by 2% or even 5%, could you still meet loan repayments?
- Terms change. Lenders can change the loan terms. For example, changing from "interest only" to "principal and interest" repayments can be a huge drain on cashflow.
- Repayment risk. What if you lose your job? Or if you lose some or all of your income because you (or your partner) become ill or injured?

And for investment loans:

- Investment income risk. What if you don't receive as much income from your investment as you expected. This could be due to a loss of income – like a property being untenanted or shares paying reduced dividends. Or it could be due to increased expenses, like significant maintenance costs on an investment property.
- Capital risk. What if the value of your investment falls and even if you sell, you won't have enough money to cover your loan balance? What if you can't sell in a timely fashion?

QUICK STEPS

- Before you buy things with credit, ensure you know what the interest rate is so you can calculate the real cost of what you're buying.
- Be wary of borrowing to invest – there is always risk involved. Seek good financial advice.
- With home loan repayments, don't be on autopilot. Work out the best use of every dollar – will that dollar create more value repaying your loan? Or contributing to super?
- If you have debts to repay, create a plan – find out the interest rate on each loan and get rid of the highest interest rate debts first.

7

CAREER: YOUR HUMAN CAPITAL

YOU ARE YOUR OWN
GREATEST ASSET – KNOW
YOUR VALUE TODAY, HOW
TO INCREASE YOUR VALUE
TOMORROW AND MAKE SURE
YOU PROTECT YOURSELF
AT ALL TIMES

◉ WORKING 9 TO 5

We recently watched a re-run of Happy Days, the 1970s sitcom version of life in the happy days of the 1950s. Mum was a homemaker, Dad had his own hardware store. The eldest son went off to the army and the main character Richie's dream was to be a journalist. There was a younger sister Joanie but we can't remember a thing about what she wanted to do.

The parents were probably in their 50s in the show, and neither showed any signs of doing anything differently career-wise. In fact, life pretty much stayed as it was – for life.

Our parents – who are now in their 70s and 80s – didn't change careers. They looked forward to retirement as soon as they could – retiring in their 60s and then enjoying their lives.

Yet if we look at people in our world, we're seeing many change tack – some as early as their 20s, many in their 40s and 50s. Kathryn returned to university in her 30s to gain her law degree, Trish in her 40s left physiotherapy to become a project manager and Michelle in her 50s re-trained to become a successful life coach.

Changing careers was once seen to be risky and somewhat foolhardy but today it's essential to refresh and re-train for what is likely to be a long working life.

UNDER PRESSURE

Your career is an essential component of your financial wellbeing.

One of the key strands in your financial tapestry is your ability to earn a sustained income over your lifetime.

Now please note that we've used the word "sustained" and that's because this is not about chasing the biggest title or the highest paying role. It's about identifying roles – which may be many and varied – in which you can continue to work and be well-rewarded.

The economists refer to this as your "human capital" – and your ability to turn this into financial capital. Your human capital is simply your earning ability over time – and will be influenced by such things as your technical knowledge and skills, your experience and expertise, and potentially your leadership, commercial acumen and entrepreneurship.

All too often people forget about the value of their human capital to weave into financial capital – and fail to sufficiently invest in themselves.

The questions we recommend that you ask yourself are these:

1. What specific goals do I have for my earnings over time?
2. What do I need to do to maximise my earning ability?
3. What risks or issues could diminish my earning ability?
4. What do I need to do to protect my ability to earn?
5. Based on my answers to questions 1 to 4, how much money will I need to invest in my earning ability over my lifetime?

PROTECTING YOUR HUMAN CAPITAL

One important way to protect your human capital is with life and disability insurance. This can help you to make sure that a possible loss of income, due to death or serious illness, doesn't knock you for six. Make sure to read the Chapter 5 on Insurance to find out more.

Career breaks and protecting your human capital value

Like many women, I took career breaks when I had my two children. The key is to make sure you are always looking after yourself and your human capital – and these apply whether it's parental leave, a study break or a career sabbatical. Of course it's also important to ensure you're keeping up when fully employed too. Here are my tips:

- While you're taking a career break, stay engaged with your team. This might mean attending any team building or strategy sessions, maybe dialling in for regular team meetings.

- Offer to do project work, paid of course. Most organisations have ebbs and flows with their workload, and an extra set of skilled experienced hands when work is flowing is highly valuable to your organisation – and keeps you in the loop.

- Keep up to speed with what's going on in your organisation and industry. Read communications and industry journals.

- Continue training. This might be completing continuing professional development or formal training programs offered by your employer or a third party provider.

- Stay connected with your network. This is more than email. This is about talking by phone or video conference, or ideally meeting in person for coffee or lunch. Even better, have ideas and insights that will add value for the people in your network.

- If you've been career focused – and would like to continue to be seen as such – then return to work full time if you can. It may be tougher initially, but the benefit is that you're not inadvertently signalling that you're no longer interested in pursuing your career. It also gives you time to re-establish yourself – which is a strong place to then negotiate flexibility if you need to.

   - Kate

Changing career

Changing careers for most people can take a few stages. Perhaps it's starting with a side-hustle, for others a similar role in an industry that excites them.

Lauren was keen to work in the music industry (and we think, who wouldn't be?). She secured a role as a legal secretary, and by building her knowledge of how the business ticked was able to jump into an account management role.

Anna was a sales consultant. For years she had been helping friends with interior design. A company restructure and redundancy payment was the ticket for Anna to make the break and formally study interior design. She set up her own interior design consultancy, and with her years of experience in sales and training in design, she is off and running.

DO THE HUSTLE: SIDE-HUSTLE

The side hustle is a popular way to earn good money and focus on your passion on the side.

You might make some extra cash but for most people it's about pursuing a passion – a chance to foray into fashion, write, create furniture or whatever you love – without quitting your day job.

It could be a way of putting a toe in the water to see if you could afford to pursue your passion full-time. Jen is in marketing, and makes and sells clothes on the side. If she could earn enough money she would love it to become her full-time hustle. And of course, you can also test how much you actually do love what you think you'll love. Writing a blog on the side might seem like a good idea but you might find that it's hard work and not really as fulfilling as you might have thought.

You will need to think about the administration and tax implications. So make sure you check with an accountant or adviser before you hustle.

Changing careers mid-career

Many mid-career women find a curious freedom, according to Joanna Maxwell, career guru and author of *Rethink your Career*. It's likely their kids are independent, they're okay financially and it's time for them to take centre stage of their own life. Don't be deterred by age.

"If you reach 50 and have a heap of fresh skills, networks, and are enthusiastic or interested then it is not gloom and doom. You could even become more specialised," Ms Maxwell writes.

Maxwell emphasises the need to be strategic. At each step, ask yourself: does this fit strategically for my career? Does it improve my human capital? Is it a growth industry that will offer opportunities for advancement and a sustained career? A job may look interesting, but you could find yourself in a dying sector. For example, the accounting profession is tipped to be undergoing an extreme shift as more core accounting services are automated. This means that accountants will need to re-shape their roles towards elements that cannot be automated, like business management and strategy.

The 5 facets of work

1. **Financial remuneration** – which is often the main reason to work, though not always the reason people stay in their jobs.
2. **Time management/structuring** – work offers a structure to our days and weeks and offers a sense of security.
3. **Socialisation** – we often underestimate the social aspect of working. Work often provides us with meaningful relationships.
4. **Status/identity** – work often provides us with a role, a place in the world.
5. **Usefulness** – a great benefit of work is to provide a sense of purpose.

    - Joanna Maxwell, Rethink Your Career.

Finding a new job

What are your main considerations in finding a new job? Money is important, so you will need to address this.

1 Prepare a cashflow plan

- Identify all of your expenses – fixed and variable. Make sure you go back and read our cashflow planning section.
- Work out what do you need to earn and if you can sustain any time where you are earning little or nothing.
- Clarify how long your savings will last.

Once you have a good idea of what you need to fund your lifestyle you can look at options in the job market.

2 Research new careers

- What do you need to have for your new career?
- What are the industry salaries – and how does this line up with the income you need?
- What is the likelihood of finding a role?
- Do you know anyone who can help give you an introduction?
- How long will it take for you to become established in the area?
- Is there a way of trialing it?

3 Decide what you want most from your new career?

- More money
- Job satisfaction
- Less stress
- Greater work life balance
- Better opportunities for the future

It might be helpful as this is a difficult question, to undertake an online values test to clarify what it is you most enjoy about work and what it is that you are likely to be best suited to, and give you greatest career satisfaction.

Choose a job you love and you will never have to work a day in your life. - Confucius.

5 tips to prepare financially for a career change

1. Prepare for left field

You can have the best plans and then something comes from left field like a health issue – or your job is made redundant. Make sure you have assets and funds to draw on if you lose your job or cannot continue working.

2. Insurance

You may have had some valuable employee benefits – including income protection, life insurance and total and permanent disability (TPD) insurance. When you are changing careers, it's important to clarify what insurance cover you have, and reassess your needs. You may be able to continue your insurances after you leave your employer (known as a continuation option). You should also ensure you know the value of these benefits so that you can consider this in your negotiations with a new employer.

3. Superannuation

This is a good time to review your super – and make sure that you don't end up with yet another super fund. Make sure you do your homework on super fund fees – as a rule of thumb, they should be 1% pa or less. If not, shop around – there will be a fund that can give you a better deal (and see the Superannuation section for more tips and information).

4. Risk

In your 20s or 30s there's less to lose so you may make riskier decisions, whereas in your 40s and 50s it's worth stepping carefully so you don't undermine what you've already established. It's about thinking about how comfortable you are to take risks and then evaluating all your decisions in the context of your goals and your comfort zone.

5. Challenge the norm

There's a lot of shoulds out there and you need to turn down the noise to make decisions that are right for you. Kate's mum was horrified when, with her two kids aged 10 and 8, she left her "secure" corporate role (in

Kate's mum's view) to start her "risky" financial advice business. Kate always felt that it was low risk – as she had the skills and experience if things didn't go to plan to step back into a corporate role. As you can see, she didn't!

So remember, someone else's idea of risk might be your idea of reward. Again, make sure to get professional help to crunch your numbers and have an objective opinion on your plans.

HOW TO GET THAT JOB THAT'S NEVER ADVERTISED: NETWORKING TO CONNECT

Whether you are looking for a job, a new job or a 180-degree career change, networking is your new best friend. Some experts say that 70% of people ended up in their current position thanks to networking.

Here's our top tips on networking to connect:

- Identify events on topics that relate to the sector in which you would like to work.
- Ask a good question of the speaker.
- When in conversation, find out how you could help someone else. Generosity goes along way when it comes to connecting.
- Once you've made a connection, follow up.
- Join an industry association and offer to roll your sleeves up and help. Most associations are thinly resourced and grateful for any assistance.
- Create a compelling LinkedIn profile – and get active by connecting with people you know (or would like to know), creating posts, commenting on other people's posts. You don't have to go anywhere for this network!

PROFILE

NAME
CHARLOTTE

AGE 51

INCOME BRACKET
$80,000-100,000

RELATIONSHIP SITUATION
MARRIED

SUPER BALANCE
$110,000

FINANCIAL ADVISER
YES

ESTIMATED PERCENTAGE OF INCOME YOU CURRENTLY SAVE - PER WEEK/MONTH/
Well actually little is saved as my salary goes to household expenses and we have to rely on my husband's for saving.

DESIRED AGE OF RETIREMENT
60

DESIRED RETIREMENT (WHAT YOU WOULD LIKE LIFESTYLE WISE)
The high life of course! Seriously, I would like to afford to go out to the theatre and dinner regularly and travel frequently. I don't feel the need for luxury travel but ideally would like to do one higher end trip each year but the rest of my travelling can be on a more modest budget. For instance, I would like to get a Eurail and do adult backpacking.

I want to be active (I will need a cure for arthritis!) and well enough to engage each day in my hobbies: ceramics, reading, going to the movies, walking and catching up with friends.

WHERE YOU ARE CURRENTLY WITH YOUR JOB/HOME/LIFESTYLE
Secondary school teacher. I work part-time on a 80% load but that translates to about 45 hours work most weeks as well as many of my holidays. I'm not so thrilled about that and would prefer to keep my job to four 10-hour days.

We own our home (with a mortgage) and intend to stay here long term as we like the area and our house suits our needs long term. It will probably need a renovation in about 10 years which we will need to save up for.

My lifestyle is too busy on the whole. I prioritise trying to do activities for my own health and social life but I do find it hard to keep up with the admin crap of life; responsibilities for older parents; read all the books I want to and keep up with all my friends!

WHAT YOU'D LIKE TO BE DOING NOW/ IN THE NEXT 5 YEARS/ IN 10 YEARS/ BEYOND

In five years I will still be working as teacher, much the same as now, but in 10 years I will be working less, travelling more, and planning retirement soon.

HOW YOU'RE PLANNING ON REACHING THERE

Actually we have a review with a financial planner underway at the moment. I want to invest some money I have sitting in a term deposit while I work out best options. Previously I owned more shares but now I am thinking of a small investment property and I need some advice of what to do about my super which is too low. I plan to have a more planned approach to planning for retirement over the next ten years.

CURRENT PRIORITIES

Spending: Some overdue house maintenance jobs like painting will use up this year's discretionary spend but otherwise will be trying to manage expenditure a bit more tightly.

Planning: actually get this in place and follow it from now on.

FINANCIAL DECISIONS YOU'VE ALREADY MADE IN LIFE TO HELP YOU ACHIEVE YOUR GOALS

Having a financial planner. Previously when I earned more money I had a personal banker who helped set up systems to ensure my earnings were always earning.

Paying off our house as a priority.

I want to invest some money I have sitting in a term deposit while I work out best options.

Making a plan to pay school fees.

When we had higher expenses associated with raising a family I engaged in active budgeting and control of expenses from pay to pay period.

FINANCIAL SITUATIONS THAT HAVE AFFECTED YOUR GOALS TO DATE

Changing my career from a lucrative one to an underpaid one! And not contributing super for many years.

Negotiating

Many women tell us that they don't feel comfortable negotiating for themselves. For most, unless they're fairly certain they will get a "yes", they are unlikely to even ask for more than is on the table.

Here are our 7 top tips for negotiating salary and rewards:

1. Know your strengths: what specific skills, experience and strengths do you offer?

2. Research the market: what is the going rate in the industry for similar roles? What are key competitors offering? What are your strengths that mean you deserve the market rate – or a premium?

3. Find out what matters most to the person you're negotiating with: perhaps they value hiring people with a certain degree or specific technical skill.

4. Make it impersonal: one useful trick is to remove the negotiation from yourself. Re-frame the negotiation so that you see the terms as having been agreed with someone else – maybe your spouse or partner – and with little discretion for you to move away from your agreed position.

5. Identify any constraints: Often a manager will have a budget for salaries for their team. There may be little point in trying for a salary raise when your company is re-structuring and offering redundancies,

6. Use time to your advantage: while you might not achieve a significant salary increase in one go, consider requesting a re-review in three or six months' time.

7. Be flexible on non-salary options. You might not get much leeway on salary, but perhaps you might get a bigger bonus percentage, the opportunity to work from home, or additional annual leave.

 **YOU CAN'T STOP THE BEAT**

Flexibility

One of the things we know from research is that most people want more flexibility in their work.

While there are many flavours of flexibility, the most common is part time work.

The RBA (Reserve Bank of Australia) reports that part-time workers (that is, individuals who work less than 35 hours per week), have become a more important share of total employment in the past 50 years. Today around one in three employed people work part time, compared with one in 10, 50 years ago.

Unsurprisingly, a striking feature of part-time work is that it has always been dominated by women – and particularly for women after the age of 30 years: "Women tend to increase their use of part-time employment as they progress through child-raising years but men do not."[1]

Now of course, child rearing is not the only reason for seeking flexibility in your work. It may be that you want flexible contract work to live out a secret dream of being a photographer or novelist, that you're caring for ageing parents, or you've simply become a travel addict and need more than four weeks' holiday a year.

When you're considering flexible work, there are a few key things to remember:

- Ensure you clarify your "guardrails" around when you're working and when you're not. Kate trialled a 4-day week for a short time and found she was working a full-time job in part-time hours – and not getting paid for it. She flipped back to full time and then negotiated additional days of leave.
- Plan for the financial implications. Part time hours means part time pay. And part time super. This is a double whammy for your financial

[1] Heath: The Evolving Australian Labour Market, 5 October 2018.

wellbeing. We recommend ensuring that you top up your super – either through additional contributions, or if you have a spouse via a super splitting arrangement.

- Gratitude should not be reflected in a lower salary. We have heard too many women say that they are just so grateful to secure flexible work that they accept a lower pay (on an hourly rate basis) than if they were to work full time. This is not a fair trade off – from experience, you will work just as hard – if not harder – and add just as much value for your part time hours as if you were full time. Think about your remuneration separately to your work schedule.

- Ask for promotions and interesting projects. Just because you work part time doesn't make you less capable. Take on the big projects, stay visible, and ensure you have a good team so you can delegate activites that require daily work attendance.

- Be creative. We believe that all work – regardless of whether you work a 67-hour week or a 37-hour week can be flexible. Create a role that you can do in your flex schedule. Find a partner to role-share. Find a new manager who needs a "wise owl" to back them – where the role is more about thought-leadership than physical presence.

- Keep up with technology. With more and more tools supporting remote working, remote teaming, project management, communications, you have the opportunity to take the lead and propose new productive ways of working to your manager, team and organisation.

Hey, perhaps you can even encourage more people to do flex work so that it becomes the "norm".

STARTING YOUR OWN BUSINESS

More and more women are starting their own businesses.

If you are starting a business, and haven't done it before maybe it's because you're risk averse. Starting your own business can be risky – and many fail. It's important to carefully consider the riskiness of your business idea before cashing in your savings to put into it. Unless you're really confident, it can be a terrifying concept.

However, if your business idea is not reliant on you putting a lot of money into it, and is just basically you going out and consulting then this is not so risky as you always have the option to return to employment. Remember to ensure that you consider your Plan B.

Education, re-education, re-skilling, re-creation

Starting over is difficult and there are many challenges and potential setbacks but it can be very rewarding.

While it might seem tempting to close one door completely while you are going through a new one, this is not always going to be a viable solution.

Firstly, financially if your new career involves significant retraining you might not be able to quit work for the period necessary to undertake all your training. If you do think about studying full-time, you need to be aware of the savings you are depleting. At this age, it may be difficult to rebuild them.

Secondly, you might need to transition from an area where you have likely built your expertise and reputation to move into an area where you will likely be starting again. It may be lonely and you may feel your worth is challenged so you might find it more bearable to ease in.

Emily is currently 52 and retraining to become a social worker. She has worked in banking since graduating from university many years ago. It has been a solid career in which she has worked through having two children, a stint working overseas following her then-husband, and taking time out in recent years to recover from breast cancer. Her interest in social work came from experience with counsellors – marriage and then dealing with cancer.

She is fortunate that her current employer has allowed her to take a career break this year to do placement work – her final hurdle in retraining for her new career.

"I thought about working another 20 years in finance and I couldn't face it, I thought I'm interested in social work so I researched requirements and available courses and enrolled – that was three years ago and I'm hoping to graduate this year. The money will be considerably less than my current job but at this time of life, I'm happy to be doing something to help others less fortunate and have a higher purpose."

A 100-year multi-stage life means we need to be better at saving, building and spending financial assets.

- In a multi-stage life, we still need to prepare for eventual retirement.
- We also need to plan and finance career breaks and career transitions. This includes re-skilling and education – as the half-life of a learned skill has already shrunk to about five years. This means that much of what you learned 10 years ago is obsolete and half of what you learned five years ago is irrelevant.
- Finally, people need to get engaged with money and finance. People can't afford to cruise along without being conscious of spending and saving.

♪ QUICK STEPS

- Create a plan for making the most of your value in the workforce – your 'human capital' – using our questions at the start of the chapter.
- Calculate how much money you will need for career breaks, refreshing and re-training. Make sure you include this in your goals and priorities.
- Check your salary. Is it in line with the median salary for your role in your industry? Should you be earning a premium?
- If you are working for a company that provides a training budget for staff, ensure you are using it to make the most of your value in the workplace – not just your current workplace but your future one as well.
- Join industry networks to give yourself good networking opportunties and ability to be tapped on the shoulder for new job openings.
- Get ready to negotiate.

8

A PLACE TO CALL HOME

TO OWN OR NOT TO OWN –
THAT IS ONLY ONE OF THE
QUESTIONS WHEN IT COMES
TO RESIDENTIAL PROPERTY
AND WHERE YOU ARE
INTENDING TO LIVE

 # YOU DON'T OWN ME

DISPELLING THE "SHOULDS"

Buying or owning a home comes with a lot of shoulds. In Australia, our culture is one where owning your home has more cachet than renting and most people (approximately 70 per cent) have purchased a home. So it's little wonder that many people believe that owning a home is money-savvy.

We want to dispel that myth. While it may make sense for some people to buy a home, it may not be the best answer for everyone. And home ownership might be perfect at some life stages, and limiting in others. There's no right or wrong about a decision to buy a home, or a decision to rent.

Don't get caught up in the world of the Joneses. Be your own Joneses. Own, rent, mix it up. The choice is yours.

Your home is an asset, but not an investment

People will often tell you that you should own a home because it is a good investment. We do believe that a home is an asset – it certainly is a thing of value. But, it's not an investment. Don't confuse the two.

Why? Because an investment is something that is expected to produce real (that is, after inflation), after-tax returns over time. Which a home does not consistently do.

If you live in your home, it is not providing an income – unlike for example the dividends from investing in shares. Unlike a usual investment, there is no cashflow benefit.

Your home may not grow in value. You might be fortunate and own a home in a time when prices are rapidly rising. However, there have been extended periods when housing prices decline. The data also shows that long run residential housing growth is fairly muted. According to the Reserve Bank of Australia data, until the 1980s, real housing prices grew broadly in line with general price inflation[1]; and since 1982, have grown at an average annual rate of around 3 per cent[2]. This compares with long run returns achieved by shares, which typically beat inflation by 5% or 6%[3].

In real life, the difference in returns is even greater. Interest on borrowings to purchase a home increases the cost. There's stamp duty on purchase, agent's fees on sale, and ongoing insurance and maintenance costs which diminish any gains on property even further. And then there's the capital cost of keeping your home up to date with the likes of new bathrooms and kitchens. And if you think that's small change, think again (see more about the ongoing costs of home ownership below).

Another important factor in considering housing as an asset but not an investment, is that housing doesn't behave like a normal investment. This is because the demand for homes is driven by a whole host of factors that have nothing to do with prospective returns. There is nothing like a new job in a new city, or a baby's impending arrival to prompt the need for a new home.

Our advice: see your home as a lifestyle asset, not an investment. If a luxury home is important to you, and you can afford it, then by all means buy a fabulous house. But if you have other priorities – overseas travel, giving your kids a head start, or taking the worry out of having enough in retirement – then don't spend a cent more on a home than you really need.

Homes are wonderful places to raise a family or entertain friends. They aren't great investments.

[1] Long Run Trends in Housing Price Growth, RBA, September 2015
[2] A Model of the Australian Housing Market, RBA, March 2019
[3] Shane Oliver, AMP Capital 'Oliver's Insights: Falling Sydney and Melbourne home prices' April 2018

Buy vs rent

We are often asked which makes more sense: buying or renting a home. As with many things at the intersection of lifestyle and financial decisions, the answer is: it depends.

It depends because your financial situation, goals, and lifestyle are unique. There's no right or wrong answer.

Kate's mum was worried when Kate decided to sell her home and rent (with two little boys in tow) many years ago. Her mum felt that renting was wasted money. But if you think about it clinically, renting is no more wasted money than interest on a home loan.

Research reveals that the cost of owning a house – which includes interest payments, repairs, rates and other running costs, less expected capital appreciation – tends to be close to the cost of renting a similar dwelling. If the cost were lower than rents, households would be financially better off owning than renting and would be expected to bid up the price of houses. Conversely, when renting is cheaper, there would be downward pressure on housing prices[4].

Your decision is more personal preference than personal finance.

It may make more sense to buy a place if:

- You expect to keep the home past a break-even period of seven to 10 years. This is because the hefty costs of buying and selling can be amortised over the life of the property – and hopefully the home has appreciated enough in value to outweigh these costs.
- You can afford a place that suits your lifestyle, and where you will feel secure and comfortable.
- You are willing and able to borrow money to buy a home.
- You like the idea of having enforced savings by repaying principal and interest on your loan.
- You value being able to stay in the one place for a long period of time.

[4]A Model of the Australian Housing Market, RBA, March 2019

Conversely, it can make more sense to rent a place if:

- Your space and/or location needs are likely to change within a period of seven years. For example, you may have teenage children where you want them to have their own bedrooms and bathroom – but you don't want to upsize, knowing that they'll be out of home in a few years' time and you'll be wanting to downsize again.
- You can't afford to buy a place that suits your lifestyle, and where you will feel secure and comfortable. You may be able to lease a place for less rent than the cost of loan interest and ongoing costs if you bought a similar home.
- Rather than taking out a home loan, you prefer to borrow for investment purposes, in which case the interest cost in may be applied as a deduction against your income.
- You are happy to set up an investment plan and invest your money into a diversified portfolio, perhaps to boost your super.
- You are open to moving if the home is no longer available to rent.

3 TIPS FOR IDENTIFYING A GOOD RENTAL PROPERTY

Here's our tips for finding a good rental place:

1. The landlord sees the property as an investment – they're not a homeowner who has re-located for a period of time. This may help secure a longer rental period.
2. The place has been well maintained. Ask the agent for records of repairs and maintenance on the property. This can help to ensure that the landlord will spend money to keep the place in good order.
3. Adjustments to the rent have been reasonable. Ask the agent or check real estate rental websites for historic information on the weekly rental.

HOW MUCH SHOULD I SPEND ON BUYING A HOME?

The ideal answer to this question is to find a home that you love, that you will feel comfortable and safe living in, but don't spend a cent more than you need to.

You may be someone with simple needs, who wishes to live in a regional area outside a major city, and so you can buy your dream home with ease.

However, for many people, the home you love is a significant stretch – and some trade-offs and clear-headed decision making is needed.

The first step is to identify what you really need for your lifestyle. At a practical level, this is working out your ideal location; proximity to transport, shops and other services; access and security; number of bedrooms, bathrooms and the other facilities you require.

Then, it's calculating your number – this is an ideal amount that you will allocate to housing out of your overall asset pool and your cashflow.

There are many "rules of thumb" that give you a ballpark amount for the price should pay for a home. This one is a useful guide:

Your total expenses on housing – including mortgage repayments and ongoing costs of maintaining your property – should be no more than 25% of your gross income. This is a very pragmatic guideline - because if you spend more than this amount on your housing costs, you simply won't have enough for your other expenses (like food and clothing which meet your basic life needs) and for your discretionary expenses which make life fun.

Next, you need to consider the costs associated with buying a home – both upfront and ongoing.

Upfront costs

The primary upfront cost to plan for is your deposit. The minimum deposit is usually 20% of the purchase price. The more money you have as a deposit, the less you will need to borrow and so the lower your loan to value ratio (LVR) will be. This is the amount of the loan divided by the purchase price (or appraised value) of the property.

If your LVR is higher than 80%, you will usually need to pay lender's mortgage insurance, and the lender could charge you a higher interest rate. It can also be very difficult to gain approval for loans with an LVR higher than 80%.

The next major cost is stamp duty, which varies by State and is typically around 4% of the property value. It's also important to tally up the smaller expenses – as they can soon add up to close to another 1%. Here's an outline of estimated costs – acknowledging that they will be different depending on where you live, the age and size of the house and the service providers you choose. We've provided two examples, one for a house valued at $750,000 and one for a house of $1,000,000.

	Amount	Percentage of house price	Amount	Percentage of house price
House price	$750,000		$1,000,000	
Stamp duty	$29,250	3.90%	$40,500	4.05%
Finance/ mortgage establishment	$1,000	0.13%	$1,000	0.10%
Legal and conveyancing fees	$1,500	0.20%	$1,500	0.15%
Removalist	$3,000	0.40%	$3,000	0.30%
Cleaning	$500	0.07%	$500	0.05%
Building and pest inspection	$600	0.08%	$600	0.06%
TOTAL	**$35,850**	**4.78%**	**$47,100**	**4.71%**

NAME
MICHELLE

ROLE
TEACHER'S AIDE

AGE 40

**INCOME
BRACKET**
<$80,000

**RELATIONSHIP
SITUATION
MARRIED WITH 2
BOYS (11 YEARS +
10 YEARS)**

**SUPER BALANCE
$115,000**

**FINANCIAL
ADVISER
NO**

**OTHER
INVESTMENTS**
None

**ESTIMATED
PERCENTAGE OF
INCOME YOU
CURRENTLY SAVE**
My pay goes straight into
paying the mortgage.
My husband's income
pays all expenses
plus savings (savings
are approximately
20% of his income,
which covers holidays,
renovations, Christmas
and unexpected medical
expenses.)

**DESIRED AGE OF
RETIREMENT**
60

**DESIRED
RETIREMENT (WHAT
YOU WOULD LIKE
LIFESTYLE WISE)**
Travel, volunteer work
(overseas and local),
outdoor activities –
hiking/bike riding, time
with my family and
friends, learn different
art/crafts, and pottering
around our home/garden.

**WHERE YOU ARE
CURRENTLY**
I work as a full-time
teacher's aide in a

Support Unit on Central
Coast of NSW. The
school is located 20
minutes from my home,
which is on a 1.5 acre
block in a beautiful valley
10 minutes from the
beach. I have a great
balance of work/family –
spending the afternoons
and school holidays with
my kids. My husband has
his own business, which is
mostly located in Sydney.
He works hard, but has
the ability to be flexible
and take time off when
needed. In our spare time
we enjoy going to the
beach, watching our kids
play sport, socialising with
friends and gardening.

**WHAT YOU'D LIKE
TO BE DOING NOW/
IN THE NEXT 5
YEARS/ IN 10 YEARS/
BEYOND**
We have just bought
a new camper trailer,
so I would really like
to explore some of
Australia. We can't afford
to do long trips away at
this stage, but we will
do short trips during
the school holidays and
weekends when we can
– while the boys are still

PROFILE

young and excited to hang out with us!

In 5 years I would like to be doing further renovations to the house and some overseas trips.

In 10 years I would like my kids to have jobs and be living independently (could be at home but in self contained area) and my husband and I to be doing some travel without the boys.

HOW YOU'RE PLANNING ON REACHING THERE

Our combined earning capacity will continue to improve and debts will become less. We would like to reduce our expenses. At the same time, we will continue to build our superannuation. It is likely that we will continue to invest in property to renovate and sell.

CURRENT PRIORITIES

Working to our new budget to maximise savings, reduce expenses and stop buying stuff

we don't need. This is a tough one and we have to be vigilant to ensure we stick to this.

FINANCIAL DECISIONS YOU'VE ALREADY MADE IN LIFE TO HELP YOU ACHIEVE YOUR GOALS

We read books which have given us some good budgeting ideas. We also recently refinanced at a lower rate – we paid off several debts and the new repayments allowed us to include savings in our new budget.

FINANCIAL SITUATIONS THAT HAVE AFFECTED YOUR GOALS TO DATE

We have bought and renovated three homes – all purchases were not in ideal market conditions, however, all properties were in good locations. We pushed our budget (and our stress levels) to ensure they were smart buys, therefore made money when it came time to sell. We also did as many of the renovations

ourselves (great to be married to a tradie).

Until recently we have sent our children to private schools but we recently made the decision to send our children to a public high school rather than private. One of our boys requires a placement in a support unit (accessed in the public system) and our younger son will attend the same school. The savings in fees will be significant. It will allow us to provide many other opportunities and experiences for them outside school. It will also reduce financial and other stress in our family which will be very welcome.

Ongoing costs

It's not just the initial costs that you need to account for when buying a home. You also need to consider the ongoing costs of maintaining your property.

We recommend doing these calculations before you buy. First, so that you can factor them into your ongoing cashflow planning. And second, so that you can clearly evaluate potential properties on a like-for-like basis. Imagine that you are lucky enough to find two properties that you love and can afford – analysing the ongoing costs of maintaining one versus the other could be the make-or-break decision on selecting which one to purchase. Even better, you may be able to use your analysis of the ongoing costs to help you negotiate (down) your purchase price.

To give you an idea of the type and amount of ongoing costs, here are some typical expenses:

	Apartment	House
House price	$750,000	$1,000,000
Contents insurance	$700	--
Home & contents insurance	--	$1,000
House & garden maintenance and upkeep	--	$10,000
Strata fees/body corporate including special levies	$7,500	--
Council and water rates	$1,000	$1,200
TOTAL	**$9,200**	**$12,200**

We hope that you're starting to see that buying a home can be an expensive decision. Not to say that it's not a good one – just that you need to factor in buying and selling costs, as well as the money you need to spend along the way.

Buying a place with someone else

Many women consider co-owning a property – for example, if they want to give an adult child a kick-start, or they would like to buy with a romantic partner.

If you're thinking about buying a place with someone else, it's important to consider carefully the financial, legal, and emotional issues before diving in.

First, you'll need to work out how you will structure the ownership of the property. There are two main options:

- **Joint Tenants:** This is the typical way that spouses own property together. Each person has equal interest in the property. From an estate planning perspective – which deals with your assets after you die – this arrangement means when one owner dies, their interest automatically passes to the other.

- **Tenants in Common:** This is a structure where each person owns a distinct share of the same property. This can be in any proportion – so for instance two people could own a place 50/50, 75/25 or 99/1. Tenants in common can be used if parties are contributing different deposits and want that to be factored in if there is property division in the future. For example, if someone contributes a $200,000 deposit and their partner adds $100,000 for a $1 million property, ownership would be split 55/45 per cent.
Tenants in common is also a good arrangement for estate planning, as you can decide who you want your share to be passed to. This is helpful when you have children from a previous relationship and wish to leave them your share of the home in your Will.
However, there is a significant risk where you have debts secured against your co-owned home. In this case, co-borrowers are jointly liable for each other's debts. If your co-owner defaults on their part of the repayments, you would have to make repayments – or suffer a bad credit rating.
It is also important for couples co-owning to realise that when it comes to a relationship breakdown, regardless of the ownership shares under

property law, the family law split can be entirely different. Even if you have set up a 75/25 split, family law is likely to see the whole asset as an asset of the relationship. In this situation, having a binding financial agreement may help (see box p155).

This is a timely reminder that you should plan for potential exits from the arrangement – either for you or your co-buyer – upfront. You can hope that it will all work itself at the time, but the reality is that when circumstances change and one partner wants out, things can turn messy.

There are 3 common reasons that people leave an arrangement:

1. Relationship breakdown – who should stay in the property?
2. One party can't meet their loan repayments.
3. One owner wishes to sell – which is particularly tricky if the other owner (or owners don't), if you want to buy them out but can't afford it, or can't agree on a price.

Before purchasing with a co-owner, it's a good idea to get advice from a solicitor. And while it sounds pessimistic, it's helpful to start by expecting a worst-case scenario. It's important to work out how you will deal with the property if you break up with your partner, have a falling out with the other owner, or have a change of circumstances that necessitates a sale.

Some people draw up a co-ownership agreement. This doesn't have to be complex, but it will require you to have rules and agreements worked out in advance. For example, co-owners may agree to have a common fund for ongoing expenses including insurance, strata/body corporate, repairs and maintenance. You may also agree upfront what happens if one wishes to sell – including whether the other co-owners have first right of refusal to buy their share and how the sale price will be determined.

You should also ensure that you update your Will once you've settled on the property – making sure you include who will inherit your share.

The best option is to buy with people with similar goals, who are in a good financial position and can meet their loan repayments and other expenses. It's a big decision – and it is worth taking the time to work through the detail, get advice from a lawyer and consider preparing a written agreement to minimise the risk of costly disputes. That way, you have the best chance of a positive outcome.

BINDING FINANCIAL AGREEMENTS

A binding financial agreement is a written document, drawn up by a lawyer, which sets out how a couple's assets will be divided if they split. There are different types, but in the case of property ownership, it can outline who will pay the mortgage and what will happen if you divide the property.

You may want to consider adding in different milestones or trigger events. For example, if you were to separate within three years, then X will happen; if you split after five years, Y will happen; if you've been together for 10 years or have a child together, then perhaps the agreement ends.

While binding financial agreements are not bulletproof, they can help to document each party's intentions at the start.

DOWNSIZING

Downsizing – which is simply where you move from a larger to a smaller home – can make a lot of sense from a lifestyle and financial perspective. A smaller property may:

- Help you release cash to repay your mortgage, or boost your retirement savings.
- Be less expensive to own – with lower costs of ongoing maintenance and upkeep.
- Reduce your utility bills. It costs a lot less to heat or cool a smaller home.

- Force you to buy less stuff – if there's no place to put it, you're much less likely to buy it.
- Offer better security – so is easier to "lock and leave" when you go away.
- Locate you closer to services and transport which would save you money (and time) in travelling from A to B.

However, we've seen some downsizer financial traps:

- Even though you're buying a smaller property, the price may not downsize. Apartments on the water or near the city often cost more than a four-bedroom house in a middle or outer suburb.
- Moving house costs. You could easily pay tens of thousands of dollars in agent's fees on your sale and in stamp duty on your purchase.
- If you're buying an apartment or town house with strata title, beware of ongoing strata fees, and body corporate special levies.
- Your furniture may not fit – nor suit – your new smaller home. You could be paying for a new fit-out.
- It's harder to entertain at home. Hosting a big family dinner might be out of the question in a smaller home – and so you may need to go out to a restaurant.
- You may not like the new experience – either the smaller space or the noise that comes with proximity to a city hub – and so you sell within a short time, again incurring costly transaction fees.

Then there are the lifestyle and emotional traps:

- What will you do with everything that won't fit into your new home?
- How will you feel leaving the house that has your life history?
- How will you feel parting with your treasures?
- What will the children think of you flogging their family home?
- How close will you be to family and friends?
- Will you feel like you've come down a notch? If a large home is important to you, then a smaller home might not fit with your values.

DOWNSIZER CONTRIBUTIONS TO SUPER

While this may be a few years away for most readers, you may be able to boost your super once you reach age 65 with a 'downsizer' super contribution. If you sell your home, if you've owned it for 10 years or more, you may be able to contribute up to $300,000 into super. You don't need to actually 'downsize' and you don't need to purchase another home. See Chapter 4 on Superannuation for more details.

TRY BEFORE YOU BUY

You usually test drive a car before you buy it and most of us try on a piece of clothing before we hand over our hard-earned cash.

Yet while buying a home is one of the biggest purchases you'll ever make, few people "try before they buy" – for instance, spending some time living in an area or in a style of property that they are thinking about buying before they commit to a purchase.

Why not apply this principle to your housing decisions? If you're thinking of moving from a house into an apartment, find a similar size and type of place and trial apartment living. If you're thinking of moving to a new area, target your ideal location and try renting for 12 months.

You might be concerned about the cost of moving, but $5,000 in moving costs is far less than $50,000 each way on a poor property purchase decision.

CONCLUSION

Think for yourself and your situation before you decide whether you want to buy a home.

Even more importantly, the decision doesn't need to be binary – play with all of the options available. You may decide to sell your current home, and take a property ownership "sabbatical". You can rent for a while, then you can buy a home that suits your next phase of life.

It's also important to debunk myths around property as a great investment. When you buy a home to live in, the data shows that this is generally not (over the long run) a money maker. Now, you may be lucky and sell your home for a profit in future. However, there are plenty of people (who never talk about it by the way) who sell at a loss.

Take the time to consider not what you think you should do, but what you really want.

MAKE SURE YOU READ OUR OTHER SECTIONS...

If you're borrowing to buy a home, you need to think about insurance – with income protection a must. Take a look at the Insurance chapter to find out more.

Many people who borrow to buy a home like to pay down their mortgage as quickly as they can. However, your other savings are also important. Read our sections on borrowing, investing and super to learn more.

How you own your home is important for how it transfers to your beneficiaries on your death. While joint tenancy automatically passes to the joint owner, 'tenants in common' relies on your wishes as outlined in your Will.

See Chapter 11 Dark Days for more.

✦ QUICK STEPS

- Do what suits you when it comes to housing. Remember buying is not always better than renting.
- When buying a home, don't over-spend. Do the numbers before you buy.
- If you're looking to rent, be choosy – check our tips in this chapter.
- If you're planning to buy a place with someone else, set yourself up for success. Get legal and financial advice at the outset.
- If you're downsizing or moving to a new area, try before you buy. It's far less expensive to rent for a year than to have to buy and sell a property.

9

RELATIONSHIPS
& MONEY

RELATIONSHIPS ARE KEY TO OUR LIFE AND IT'S IMPORTANT WHO WE CHOOSE TO PARTNER WITH ESPECIALLY WHEN WE'RE PLANNING OUR FUTURE

⦿ FOR THE LOVE OF MONEY

Relationships are key to our life and it's important who we choose to be our partner and peers. Especially if you're trying to save and get ahead. That's because many of the choices we make – where we live, the car we drive, the places we dine – are influenced by who we spend time with.

If you don't think friends influence your spending habits, consider this: Have you ever spent more than you planned on a night out so you wouldn't feel left out? Have you felt pressured into spending more on a holiday or weekend away with friends? Most of us have. As we get older and wiser, we usually learn to make better choices with our money, and not give in to financial peer pressure.

MARRIAGE: LET'S STICK TOGETHER

We've interviewed many women, and those at the top in their field nearly always say that their choice of partner is key to their success. There are also many we spoke to who sacrificed their relationship on their way up the ladder – either willingly or because they uncovered a difference in values.

In terms of financial responsibility in relationships, studies indicate that in most heterosexual couples women are more likely to have primary responsibility for the day-to-day family finances while men are more likely to take the lead on investing[1]. However, Australian research shows that the more highly educated and higher paid the woman, the less likely she is to be in a relationship where the male is the main decision maker[2].

---

1 https://www.hsbc.com/media/media-releases/2018/half-of-women-around-the-world-fear-they-wont-be-able-to-afford-food-in-retirement

2 https://australiancentre.com.au/publication/who-makes-the-financial-decisions-intra-household-evidence-from-panel-data/

Where do you stand?

If you're the one who is not leading nor engaged in financial and investment decisions, you may be losing confidence in your own financial knowledge. It's time to start taking an active interest.

If you are the lead decision-maker, then it's time to ensure your spouse is in the loop – with both day-to-day cashflow, and major spending and investment decisions. Remember you're in this together – for better or for worse!

Don't expect that you will agree on everything. Research suggests that more than two-thirds of couples disagree on significant financial decisions. Do read Chapter 1- Values, Goals & Priorities to help you clarify what's most important to you, how you're going to navigate your differences and have the best chance of achieving your goals.

9 QUESTIONS FOR YOUR NEXT DATE

Whether you're in a long term relationship, or starting a new one, here are 9 questions for your next date.

1 Did you have money as a kid? How did you earn it? What did you do with it?

2 Were your parents spenders or savers?

3 If you won $1 million today, what would you do with it?

4 Of my money-habits, which do you like the most?

5 What does having money mean to you?

6 What would it take for you to feel happy about money?

7 When it comes to money, what worries you?

8 What are you comfortable telling me about your money? Any debts that are important to know?

9 What dreams do you have that you need money to achieve? What are your plans to achieve them?

And of course, if you need help, reach out to a financial adviser. A good adviser is like a personal coach – an objective professional who works with you to give you options to reaching your goals. As much as you might like to achieve all of your goals, often trade-offs need to be made. A financial coach can be impartial and offer good guidance. Ultimately of course, it's you who has to decide and act.

Protecting your assets

Many people are concerned about a relationship ending – whether de facto or marriage – and being able to separate assets that they have created or inherited prior to entering a new relationship.

One of the few legal ways to do this is to establish a pre-nup – formally known as a binding financial agreement. This is a legal document through which you determine what happens to your assets if you separate. While lawyers caution that they are not bullet-proof, a properly prepared financial agreement may take some of the stress out of splitting.

Each party to the agreement must seek independent legal advice on how the agreement affects their rights and whether it is to their advantage or not. Each lawyer must also provide a signed document confirming that legal advice was given. The financial agreement doesn't need to be approved by a court. While it's a good idea to have it set up before you enter a relationship, you can also create a binding financial agreement when you're already together or even during separation.

Another option for protecting assets relates to helping your children financially. Instead of giving your children money, you can provide a loan. Lawyers will typically recommend documenting the loan in writing including terms like the amount of interest and regular repayments and having all parties sign the loan agreement. Parents may also wish to secure the loan through a registered mortgage over the child's property. Again, it is important to seek help from a legal professional.

BINDING FINANCIAL AGREEMENTS: THE FINE PRINT

A Binding Financial Agreement states how your assets, financial resources and liabilities will be divided if your relationship breaks down. It may include:

- What happens to any property you bring into the relationship if you break up
- What happens to any debts you already owe
- What happens with assets or liabilities you acquire either separately or jointly during the relationship
- How assets that you jointly own, including bank accounts, would be divided
- Who pays the mortgage and on what terms
- What happens if one of you no longer earns an income
- What happens to any pets you may have together

It must be in writing and must refer to the relevant section of the Family Law Act 1975. It must be signed by all parties, and before the agreement is signed, each party must obtain their own independent legal advice. The lawyers they consult must give advice addressing specific matters set out in the legislation and then sign the required certificate. A copy of the certificates signed by each of the lawyers must be provided to both parties.

Marriage and your Will

Did you know that when you marry your Will becomes invalid? The only time where this doesn't apply is if you made a Will before marrying that states it is made "in contemplation of marriage". This is particularly important if you have children from a previous relationship or have other specific intentions for your assets if you die. Either way, it is a good idea to prepare a new Will if you marry.

DIVORCE: SHOULD I STAY OR SHOULD I GO?

Arguments about money are the top predictor for divorce – and it doesn't matter about wealth or education. Money arguments are more intense, last longer and take longer to recover from.

If you – or your partner – decide it's time to go, there are some important things to consider. While the law on marriage and de facto matters varies state-by-state in Australia, there are some fundamentals that are the same.

Firstly, when you are married, your marriage begins the day you are married and your separation is official a year after you separate. For de facto relationships, although all the rules remain the same as marriage under the Family Law Act, the dates are less simple to establish. De facto is often said to start two years after the relationship begins but definitions and dates can be unclear. We like the definition used by some lawyers called the "toothbrush" test: that is if you're leaving your toothbrush at your partner's place and they're doing your washing from time to time, then chances are you're in a de facto relationship. In other words, you don't have to be living in the same residence to be in a de facto relationship.

What assets are in or out?

One of the most common questions we're asked is what assets are counted in the mix.

The answer is everything that is in either spouse's name, both spouses' names and all assets that are under either partner's control (for example via a trust). The assets will usually include your home, superannuation, investments, bank accounts, cars and anything else of value like artwork or jewellery. Now, most people undergoing a relationship separation focus on the assets. It's also critical to clarify your debts. If you have loans in joint names, then you are jointly responsible. However, once you've separated you're not responsible for your partner's debts just because of your relationship. Where you might find yourself liable however is if you signed a loan contract as a joint borrower or guarantor; or you were a director of a family company or partner in a business. In this case, the best option is to have your partner re-finance the loan. You need to be mindful that a property settlement (via the courts) does not have the power to divide debts or change your contract with a lender (whether you are the borrower, or guarantor of a loan).

In splitting the assets it's also important to consider the future income needs to service debts and cover potential childminding costs. An expert financial adviser will be able to help you navigate estimated costs in this area.

In addition, family law matters are complex, and it is best to seek advice from a specialist family lawyer.

FINANCIAL VS NON-FINANCIAL CONTRIBUTION

When a court divides property it takes into account both people's financial and non-financial contributions to the relationship. For example, it will look at the division of household labour and , if you have children, the contribution you've both made as a parent. It will also take into account the amount of money both you and your former partner earned and will consider any differences in your future earning capacity and your obligations to care for the children.

Source: Law Society of NSW

SEPARATION: FIRST STEPS

1 Protect your privacy: Change passwords for your computer, mobile phone, internet and phone banking, phone or internet plans and social media.

2 Record key dates: Including date of separation which can help when you apply for a property settlement and/or divorce as proof that you have been separated for at least 12 months.

3 Clarify your financial position:
• Do a financial stocktake – list all your assets, and any debts or joint debts in your name (you can use the MoneySmart asset stocktake calculator – link on p169).
• Ask your bank for the past seven years of statements (you may need these in the future) and make sure that you are receiving email statements for current bank accounts and loans.
• See your bank about ways to protect your money and ensure any loans don't increase.

4 Re-set your bank accounts, credit cards and loans so you can access funds and control loans:
• Close joint accounts. Move your share to your own bank account, or use the money to pay joint debts.
• Ensure you have a bank account in your name where only you have access. Have your pay go into this account.
• Re-set your joint home loan. Inform your loan provider of your separation, re-set the signing authority to "both to sign". If your home loan has a redraw facility or linked credit card, cancel these options. Re-finance or repay the loan as soon as possible.
• Cancel joint credit cards repay any amounts owing.
• Set up your own credit card – ideally before you separate.

5 Change your rental agreement if you're moving out and your partner is staying. Arrange with the landlord to be released from the rental agreement – or you could be liable for rent or any damage caused by your partner after you leave. You may also have to apply to get your bond returned or transferred.

6 If you own property in joint names, seek advice from a solicitor. In particular, if property is held in your partner's name, you need to ensure it is not sold before the property settlement.

7 Update utility bills and other subscription services including electricity, gas, phone, internet, streaming services. If your name is on the account, then you are liable for any unpaid accounts.

8 Gather other essential documents. Review the separation checklist (see link below) as a guide for things to do, consider, gather or action.

9 Contact Centrelink: Your change in relationship status may qualify you for some government assistance, so inform Centrelink as soon as you can.

10 Update your Will and death benefit nominations. Separation doesn't impact your Will – and so if you die, your spouse may inherit assets (or if they are your Executor, have control of your estate) even though you may not want them to. Divorce does affect your Will, but it does so differently in each state and territory. Depending on where you live, it may make your Will invalid or could simply revoke your former spouse as your executor or any gift left to them. You should also check your death benefit nominations for your super fund, and for any life insurance policies.

11 Prepare to apply for property settlement. If you have applied for divorce, once this is final, there is a time limit of 12 months to apply to the court for property settlement or spousal maintenance. If you don't apply within this time you need leave of the court – and it's better if you don't end up in this this situation as there are circumstances where leave may not be granted.

12 Seek financial advice. A good adviser can help you to clarify your current financial position and work with your lawyer to navigate your property settlement.

www.moneysmart.gov.au/tools-and-resources/calculators-and-apps/asset-stocktake-calculator

www.moneysmart.gov.au/life-events-and-you/life-events/divorce-and-separation/divorce-and-separation-financial-checklist

Sources: ASIC Money Smart; Westpac Separation Hub (2019).

RE-MARRIAGE AND RE-PARTNERING: JUST LIKE STARTING OVER

Re-marriage or re-partnering often comes with complications. One or both of you may have children, property, investments or liabilities.

Most people are very concerned to protect the assets they bring into a new relationship.

Before you take the step of moving in together or getting married, have an honest conversation about money, values and goals.

Know your position and what you're bringing to the relationship. Equally make sure you know what your partner is bringing – most importantly – make sure you know if there is debt, or crippling payments that need to be made to previous partners and children.

Then once you have a shared knowledge of your combined position think about formalising your position in case your relationship breaks down at a later date. It's better to be safe than sorry. This is where a Binding Financial Agreement (discussed earlier) could help.

SEXUALLY TRANSMITTED DEBT: TAINTED LOVE

What a wonderful phrase – and what a pity it so well expresses such a nasty issue. Coined in Australia in the early 1990s, "sexually transmitted debt" is where a debt is passed from one person to their romantic partner – so that they become responsible for their partner's debts often without realising their risk or responsibility.

And it seems that it's more often women who are vulnerable to sexually transmitted debt as they feel an obligation to support their partner, and may feel that they have to sign for something they may not otherwise take on.

Some common examples include where a husband runs his own company and asks his wife to guarantee the business loan from the bank. Or it could be that one partner has a poor credit rating and is unable to secure a car loan, and even though the car is registered in his name, the loan is taken out in his wife's. If he leaves and takes the car, she is responsible for repaying the loan.

Here's some ways that you can protect yourself:

- Avoid guaranteeing a loan or a credit card.
- If you break up and any bills are in joint names, tell your providers immediately. Ensure you keep records in writing.
- If you have joint loans, tell the bank. Again, make sure you have your instructions in writing.
- Even better, don't agree to or sign anything without getting legal advice. In particular, be careful about being asked to sign a loan document as a witness – as you could be really signing as a co-borrower.

Remember: ignorance is no excuse.

FINANCIAL ABUSE – RUN FOR YOUR LIFE

Cathy, now in her 50s, took time out from her career as a nurse to support her husband Dan and raise two children. She experienced financial abuse – but it was so gradual and invisible to the outside world that she didn't quite believe it was happening.

- He controlled all the bank accounts – Cathy had no access.
- He provided Cathy with cash for household and kids' expenses. He called it her pocket money like she was a child.
- She wanted to return to work when the kids were in their teens. He didn't want her to work, so he cut her allowance so she didn't have enough money to pay her bus fare to get there.
- He did not share with her any information about their finances.
- He excluded her in financial decisions, telling her she wasn't equipped to make money decisions.
- He pushed away other relationships, so her friends did not want to be around.

These are just some of the signs of financial abuse in an intimate relationship – including controlling access to money, and a partner's ability to earn. Cathy's story reminds us that it can happen to anyone, regardless of education, wealth or age.

For more information go to:
https://www.womenandmoney.org.au/what-is-financial-abuse

PAY ATTENTION TO MONEY AND YOUR RELATIONSHIP

If you don't pay attention to money in your relationship, it can tear you apart. If you don't talk about your finances, you can very quickly find yourselves fighting about how the other spends money. You use money every single day. It affects everything from where you live to what you have for breakfast. So, whether you like it or not, it's going to affect the way two people who are sharing their lives co-exist with one another.

So take the time to pay attention to money in your relationship, make sure you regularly and actively discuss your finances so that it doesn't cause unnecessary friction and slowly tear you apart.

 QUICK STEPS

- Set up a weekly money meeting – where you set aside time to talk about your money and financial decisions.
- Clarify your priorities – work your way through our chapter on values, goals and priorities.
- Get on the same financial page – use our SASSY framework to ensure you have a clear picture of your current cashflow and assets and liabilities, and then set up structures to support you. (The more you develop structures upfront, the less you're likely to debate!)
- If you're worried about protecting assets from a potential relationship breakdown, get a Binding Financial Agreement. It's never too late.
- If you're splitting, check our "first steps" in this chapter.
- Beware sexually transmitted debt: don't sign any loan documents you don't 100 per cent understand.
- If you're concerned about financial abuse – for you or a friend – get expert help immediately.

10

MONEY & KIDS

OUR FAMILIES ARE THE REASON MOST OF US WORK – ENSURING THAT WE ARE PREPARED FOR WHAT'S NEXT IS VITAL IN SETTING UP OUR FAMILIES FOR THE FUTURE

# WE ARE FAMILY

For most people, money is not just about themselves. They want to help their children and can often sacrifice their own priorities to see their children get ahead.

But there's a balance. We found in our research for this book that the people who are well-positioned financially now had to earn money, manage money and make trade-offs about spending and saving when they were kids.

So, if you want to raise financially fit adults, then get them exercising their financial muscles early.

Here are some ideas:

- Assign them money-earning chores to earn a weekly allowance. Ideally, these are extra jobs beyond the day-to-day tasks (like cleaning their room or setting the table) needed to contribute to family life.
- Agree an amount of this weekly allowance for their "spending" and an amount for their "fun" account (which they can use to buy special items like toys and games) and a portion for long-term savings. You may notice that this is exactly the same as the adult accounts we recommended in our SASSY framework. Train those muscles early!
- When they receive money for birthday or Christmas presents, also have an agreed amount that goes into each account.
- When they want to buy something special, ask them to write it down on a "wish list" and when they have enough spending money and "fun" money, they can buy it.
- Talk to them about how to make the most of their money. Can they buy the toy they want on special? Instead of buying a book, can they borrow it from the library or online library?
- For friends' birthday gifts, agree a budget for how much they can spend.
- Show them how much they have saved in each of their accounts – and celebrate when they achieve milestone amounts.

CHRISSY'S STORY

Chrissy, mother of one, age 50, says that the compelling drive to support her son dictates almost all her current decisions and choices. Her partner works part-time so, as primary breadwinner she feels the burden is more on her.

"I'm torn between giving the long-lasting intangible (and costly) benefits of quality education and experiences such as travelling together versus the bottom line benefit of financial assets," she said.

"It's important that we've set him up well, particularly through education. I see this as a positive way of sharing with him what I've been able to achieve through my own struggles. But as a child of migrants, I'm also driven by a fear that I won't be able to leave him enough. So that creates a compulsion to continue to work hard, save hard, accumulate, and build on the small amount I was given by my own family so he can have an easier life.

"At some point I will feel I've done enough, that I have invested a great deal in work, often at great sacrifice, to achieve what I have. I'm working towards getting my son through school and established at uni before I pack it in and either slow down or adopt a much healthier work life balance. And ultimately that will be my point of 'I've done what I can. Now is my time.' It might be in two years or it may be slightly longer, but I feel that the current pace I'm working is unsustainable for the long-term."

PROFILE

NAME
AGNETHA

AGE 50

**INCOME
BRACKET
>$180,000**

**SUPER BALANCE
$200,000**

**FINANCIAL
ADVISER
NOT AT THE
MOMENT**

RELATIONSHIP SITUATION

Partner of 22 years. For the most part, she manages the finances. I work long hours in a job that is mentally taxing, and watching the bills makes me anxious. We have a joint account that we barely touch. She takes charge with most of the finances.

SUPER BALANCE

I have three funds that I've recently consolidated into two. One is a retail fund, the other is a corporate fund because its Death and disability insurance is good and it provides medical benefits for my family. Without those benefits, I'd consolidate into one fund to pay less in fees.

OTHER INVESTMENTS

We live in my partner's home which is paid off. I have two investment properties valued about $2.4 million, with $500,000 debt. I rent one for a good income which pays off that mortgage. The other is a split level house and my parents live in the bottom part. I obviously don't charge them rent and I pay bills and the mortgage myself.

ESTIMATED INCOME CURRENTLY SAVED

We don't have a lot of disposable income. Much of it goes to private school fees/child costs, and the mortgages.

I would probably save about $1,500 a month.

DESIRED AGE OF RETIREMENT

55-58

DESIRED RETIREMENT LIFESTYLE

Travel extensively. Sell our house and rent or buy a city apartment with some views.

WHERE YOU ARE CURRENTLY

I work full-time on a contract basis.

Lifestyle is very low key. School fees are costing us about $32,000 a year, plus extras of about $8,000.

I buy clothes during the sales, and only when I really need them. I don't buy books anymore – I borrow them from the library. I also listen to free podcasts (crime rocks!) and have the free version of Spotify.

I negotiate mobile phone arrangements and I work out the best value for the least amount of money based on usage.

I encourage my son to keep track of his pocket money – he has to pay $10 towards his mobile phone bill, and $10 to a charity of his choice (he chose to sponsor an orangutan through WWF).

Our sole indulgence is travel. We like to stay in good places. I negotiate directly with the hotels to get the best price. We walk everywhere and eat one meal a day for the most part. We don't skimp on food and we select our indulgences – for example we were in New York for Christmas one year and indulged in Christmas lunch at the Waldorf Astoria – a dream of mine.

We've seen loads of shows – theatre and musicals. I find out where to find value for money, where the best places are, half price tickets for shows etc.

HOW YOU SEE YOUR FUTURE

After my son finishes school, I'd like to cut back work to four days a week. I'll keep paying off the properties although by then they'll be reduced and the burden will be less.

Beyond that, I would like to travel extensively. My ultimate goal is to travel for six months of the year – live in a village or town for several weeks or months at a time to enjoy the local life.

My partner has a condition linked to weather and can't function in cold environments. So we will probably aim for endless summers.

YOUR PLANNING TO GET THERE

Find alternative sources of income. I've just applied for freelance work to help with expenses. I plan to work hard for the next few years and keep investing where I can in super. With property the maintenance costs are high and I don't want the mistake of putting all my eggs in one basket.

I've also started paying more close attention to my super investment options, and will start salary sacrificing from next financial year.

I've also started paying more close attention to my super investment options, and will start salary sacrificing from next financial year.

MONEY AND KIDS IN BLENDED FAMILIES

Most of us remember the Brady Bunch – and in the 1970s the blended family was still the exception not the norm. Today, it's not unusual at all. Although, if we were living next door to Carol and Mike and housekeeper Alice and the six kids, we would still probably find them a little unusual.

If you have children and then re-partner, you'll need to decide how you manage the inevitable expenses in the upbringing of children. If you're divorced, then you'll probably have to set up workable money arrangements with the kids' other parent. If you have children from your previous relationships and then have children together, things are going to be trickier.

Whatever your situation, here are just a few financial considerations.

• What is your approach to schooling? Will each child have the same type of schooling – private school, public school? Primary and secondary?

• How much money will be set aside for extracurricular activities?

• How will day-to-day living expenses for the children be shared – particularly if one of you has children and one doesn't; or one has more children than the other; or one partner's children have more time living with you?

• How much will you budget for gifts for each child for birthdays, Christmas, and other special events?

• What happens where one partner has spousal or child maintenance obligations to a former partner?

• What is your approach to pocket money?

It's essential to discuss matters at the outset – this can be a very emotional and divisive issue in a blended family relationship. Of course, ideally you want to treat all the children equally, but we know from personal experience that sometimes that's just not possible. The best bet is to set up your guidelines early. Decide on the issues that are really important and the things that you can let ride.

NOT QUITE INDEPENDENT ADULT CHILDREN

Your children are your children forever and you will probably want to help them at all stages of their lives. Even once they've finished school, it's likely that your kids could still use a helping hand financially. Maybe they're studying at college or university, maybe they're living independently and need some help with living expenses or just a short term top-up to tide them over from time to time.

However, you will also have two competing objectives: you need to look after your own financial wellbeing, and you need to raise financially fit children.

Here are some suggestions for your emerging-adult children and money:

- Help them create their own cashflow – so that they begin to understand the cost of living.
- Encourage and support them in getting a job they enjoy – casual or part time if they're studying; full time if they're ready to work.
- If they're living at home, require that they pay board. Even if you put this money into a separate account with the intention that you will give it back in future – it is a great way to create forced savings.
- If you're supporting them financially – for example, if they're living out of home and studying – instead of paying their bills for them, provide them with an allowance so that you are not a boundless ATM and they have to learn to manage their money.

MOSTLY INDEPENDENT ADULT CHILDREN

Another area that comes up for many parents is wanting to help their children with a financial boost – whether it's to buy a property, start a business, or tide them over during troubled times.

We believe you should proceed with care:

- You first need to look after your own financial wellbeing – as the airlines say, put on your own oxygen mask first. Do the numbers to work out if you can afford to help your children – or if you need to focus on helping yourself. A financial adviser can assist you with this type of scenario modeling.

- You need to protect any money you provide from things like a relationship breakdown, a failed business or bankruptcy (see box below).

- Consider offering a short term loan – particularly if you want to them to stay accountable for their expenses. You can structure a loan, even if it's on favourable terms, with the strict intention that interest is paid and the principal is repaid within a given time. We call this the "family bank" – and we've shared some examples in the "Borrowing Money" chapter so take a look.

ENSURING YOUR MONEY IS PROTECTED

You want to make sure your money is protected. So if you are going to give your child a hand it may be best not to hand over any money as a gift – and instead use a loan. This can be particularly helpful if your child is in a relationship and you don't want the funds to become part of a family law split. Where money is provided as a loan, you can ask for it be repaid to you if that relationship breaks down. Otherwise, your money will become part of their community property and half may be given to the partner who they are no longer with. It's a good idea to consult a lawyer about drawing up a loan agreement.

THE NEXT GENERATION – GRANDCHILDREN

A long-term option to financially help the next generation – and protect your family's assets along the way – is to establish testamentary trusts in your Will.

In this case, rather than giving a beneficiary their inheritance outright, their entitlement is held in trust. You can set this up so that trust assets can only pass to blood descendants – that is, your children and grandchildren.

Without this type of testamentary trust, a number of circumstances can put your child's inheritance at risk. The inheritance can be squandered by your son- or daughter-in-law, grandchildren from your child's first marriage could be disinherited by a son- or daughter-in-law from a second marriage.

The trustee has the discretion to pay all or part of the funds held in the trust to the beneficiary or to the beneficiary's dependents in such amounts and at such times as the trustee decides.

To find out more, read Chapter 11 Dark Days.

 QUICK STEPS

- Put in place simple steps to teach your children how to make money, manage money and make decisions about spending and saving – our tips in this chapter for each age and stage are a good start.
- Before helping adult children, do your numbers to ensure you're financially okay.
- Use a structured loan to help your kids and keep them accountable for their spending.
- If you're helping with a significant sum, create a loan (rather than a gift) to protect your assets.

11

DARK DAYS

DEATH IS NOT WHAT WE
WANT TO THINK ABOUT –
WHICH IS WHY WHEN IT
HAPPENS TO SOMEONE
CLOSE WE ARE OFTEN
UNPREPARED AND UNABLE
TO MANAGE EFFECTIVELY

◎ WHEN DOVES CRY

When someone dies there's generally a panic, a feeling of loss and a sort of paralysis, especially when it is unexpected. For most people, when you are confronted by this kind of shock and great loss it is best to leave any major life decisions until you return to your more normal self. This can be up to a year and sometimes even longer. Don't rush to move house, change cities, give things away, or start a new relationship until you are truly ready and your mind is clear.

Once you're in your 40s, it is more likely that the cause of death will be chronic illness while the leading causes of death for younger people are external causes, such as accidents and suicides[1].

With a chronic illness, most people will be more focused on their health and medical treatment than estate planning. And some leave their estate planning too late, which is why you should put a plan in place early, said Geoff Stein, partner Brown Wright Stein Lawyers.

"Try to encourage consultation. Who is it in the family group that needs to be looked after? Who will take responsibility? If husbands and wives are each other's executors who's the substitute if they can't do it and will that person provide the necessary moral support?" said Stein.

"Where will the money be coming from to cover debts? Who will pay for funeral expenses? An average funeral can cost between $5,000 and $25,000 and not everyone has access to that money, although many service providers in that area will wait until the probate clears on the deceased's estate."

Some people procrastinate about preparing their Will. Which is not surprising if you consider that preparing your Will is one of the most revealing aspects of your life. It reveals who and what you really care about – and at the end of the day can't hold any secrets – because it is the **last Will and testament** which means after it is enacted there is no comeback. You will no longer have a say from beyond the grave.

[1] www.aihw.gov.au/reports/life-expectancy-death/deaths-in-australia/contents/leading-causes-of-death

Don't delay. All individuals aged 18 or older should have a Will. Ask a legal professional to help you draw up your plan.

ESTATE PLANNING IS NOT JUST FOR THE WEALTHY

Typically a financial adviser, a lawyer and an accountant will work together to help you design an estate plan that enables you to say how you want your assets distributed after your death – as well as how you will be looked after, financially and medically, if you're so unwell that you can't make decisions for yourself.

What makes up your estate plan?

An estate plan is more than just your Will. Other key documents might include:

- Superannuation death benefit nominations
- Insurance policy death benefit nominations
- Powers of attorney
- Power of guardianship
- Advance Care Directive
- Testamentary trusts

You'll notice that your super and insurance policies are noted as being separate to your Will – this is because these policies sit outside your Will and the beneficiaries named in those policies will override anyone mentioned in your Will. If you own property as joint tenants, this is also outside your Will – your share will pass automatically to the other party (tenants-in-common is covered by your Will). Also if you have a family trust, the trust is separate to your Will – it continues on and its assets will also be distributed according to the trust deed, not anything written in your Will.

1 The Will

This will determine where your money and investments are spread after your death. You need to think very carefully about this. While DIY Will kits can record your basic intentions, once there are any complications – like divorces, unclear splitting of assets, or additional dependents you may not have yet updated – these Wills might not provide you with the result you intended.

A lawyer is trained to ask you the questions necessary to make your intentions very clear. Your lawyer can't make your decisions so before you go to see your lawyer you need to have a think about where you want your money to go.

A very smart lawyer once gave me this great advice when you are thinking about your Will: sit down with some blank pages of paper, a pencil, a glass and a bottle of wine.

- First, pour yourself a glass of wine.
- Start writing down where you think you want your assets to go – who inherits?
- Then, consider one of those people is no longer alive when you die. What would you like to do now?
- Have some more wine, turn the page and start again.
- Consider, that your next choice won't be an option either.
- Turn a new page, have some more wine, and start thinking about that option.
- Then keep repeating.

Now, this may seem excessive, both in terms of wine consumption and planning but in our experience, most people face a dilemma or two in working out their Wills.

"I had a surprisingly difficult situation with my parents – even though everything at first seemed very simple. As an only child my parents wanted to leave everything to each other and to eventually pass to me. Their lawyer asked, "what if Julia is no longer around?". This was confronting for my parents," Julia said.

"It became difficult as my parents felt they were splitting the estate with people they didn't really want it to go to – and this is where I realised the wine is a good idea. As the decision becomes more distant and remote in likeliness it's a good idea to feel a little more distant and remote and not get caught up on little things, like your brother's daughter was rude to you a few years ago, or you don't really like your nephew's wife. And at the end of the day, you're dead anyway!"

A Will may automatically become invalid if you get married, divorced or if it is not signed or witnessed properly. It is also important that you update the document when there are births, deaths, marriages, and divorces in the family. You must avoid mistakes when you are writing a Will and it is recommended that you update your Will when there is a major change to your family, or every three years – even if just to make sure the people you've named are still around and that you're still happy with your choices.

WHAT HAPPENS IF I DON'T HAVE A WILL?

- If you die without a Will, assets are divided between family members according to the law – which could mean that your assets don't go to the people you planned.
- There is no executor, so an administrator must be appointed. Applying to the court for letters of administration is similar to applying for probate of a Will, but could add cost and complexity to the process.
- You miss the opportunity to put structures in place to protect assets and to minimise unnecessary tax.

2 Testamentary trusts

A Testamentary Trust is a special type Trust that is only created when the individual Will-maker dies. They can be beneficial in protecting assets and in tax planning – particularly when it comes to the tax paid by minor beneficiaries (that is, children under age 18).

They can help to protect the deceased's assets because where there is a Trust in place, the assets belong to that Trust rather than to any individual. This makes it more difficult for the assets to be accessed by creditors or divorcing partners. However, be aware that they are not bullet proof.

From a tax perspective, the Trustee (or Trustees) can also choose to distribute the income generated by the Trust in a way that manages tax. In particular, children under the age of 18 can receive income at adult marginal tax rates (including accessing the tax-free threshold) which can be very valuable from a financial planning point of view. You can't do this with ordinary family trusts (in this case minor children can be taxed at more than the highest adult marginal tax rate).

There is a cost to including a Testamentary Trust in your Will – which could be an additional amount of between $2,000 and $5,000. A standard Will may cost between $600 and $5,000 depending on the complexity.

Testamentary trusts are particularly popular where individuals have substantial assets, subsequent marriages and blended families.

3 Superannuation death benefit nominations

You want to nominate a superannuation beneficiary so you can effectively tell your super fund who you'd like your super money to go to. Importantly, only particular relationships can receive your super benefit:

- your spouse (including de facto and same sex partners), but not former spouses
- your children regardless of age (including step children)
- anyone who is financially dependent on you when you die
- your estate or legal personal representative.

You may wish to nominate your estate or legal personal representative as this directs funds to your Will – and you can then specify in your Will how and to whom you want your super money paid, including the types of beneficiaries above as well as other people in your life.

4 Life insurance beneficiary nomination

If you own a life insurance policy personally (not through super), you will have been asked to nominate who you would like to receive this money when you die. Unlike super, there are a wide array of people who you can nominate. It can make it quicker and easier for your loved ones to receive the payment. If you don't nominate a beneficiary, your life insurance benefits will be paid to your estate and will be distributed according to your Will, if you have one.

5 Powers of Attorney

Powers of attorney operate during your life and enable you to formally appoint someone you trust to make decisions on your behalf if you're unable to do so in property and financial matters.

There are two main types:

- The first is a general power of attorney which is usually given for a specific time, for example, if you will be travelling overseas. It ceases if you lose capacity – that is, the ability to make your own decisions.
- That's when the second type kicks in. This is called an enduring power of attorney – and it enables your nominated attorney to make decisions when you can no longer do so.

Who should you nominate? Someone you absolutely trust – because as your attorney, they will be able to do anything you could do with your property and money. Some people appoint more than one person – and can say whether they require them to agree and decide jointly or whether one individual can act independently of the others.

6 Power of Guardianship

This is where you appoint someone to make lifestyle, health and medical decisions for you when you're unable to do so. Often called an Enduring Guardian, this person can decide such things as your medical care and where you live.

7 Living Will: Advance Care Directive and Advance Health Care Directive

You may have heard this called a "Living Will". It is a document you use to provide specific instructions about your medical care and your "end of life" choices. This document doesn't have a set format, nor require witnesses. So if you want to make an Advance Care Directive you can simply write down your wishes and include this with your other estate planning documents.

WHAT HAPPENS WHEN A BUSINESS PARTNER DIES?

If you're in business with a partner, it's essential that you engage in succession planning to minimise difficulties down the track. This should include what you'd like to happen if one partner wants to exit the business, becomes unable to work due to illness or injury or dies.

Many business partners take out insurance for the value of each other's share of the business so that the business will continue with the remaining partner(s). Ideally you will also have undertaken a buy/sell agreement where you and the partner(s) and perhaps spouses enter into an agreement to negotiate terms and conditions of transfer of ownership in the event of death or permanent disability.

It is important that you consider in your ownership agreement as if the deceased's share becomes part of their estate, running the business may prove difficult in the future if you find yourself with new co-owners without the skills, interest or same values.

PUTTING PAPERWORK TOGETHER

When someone dies, a doctor must sign a certificate that confirms the death. Funeral arrangements cannot be made until the doctor has signed and issued this certificate. It is generally called a Doctor's Certificate of Cause of Death. The funeral company can then take the deceased into their care.

The Death Certificate will also help you access:

• bank accounts

• centrelink details

• utilities and other payment accounts

• superannuation

• other investments

• tax records

• social media accounts.

Insurance policies

At this time, sometimes private health, sickness, accident or life insurance policies may help pay funeral and other expenses. If you think a person who died had insurance, call the company and ask if they can help.

CO-OWNING A PROPERTY – WHAT HAPPENS WHEN ONE PERSON DIES?

How you own a property – as tenants-in-common or joint tenants – will impact the transfer of ownership when a co-owner dies.

• With joint tenants, when one owner dies, their share automatically passes to the other owner (or owners). This is most common in marriages.

• With tenants-in-common, when one owner dies, their share is passed to those nominated in their Will.

The funeral

Funeral costs will vary between around $5,000 and $25,000 on average but can cost much more depending on choice of headstone, cemetery and coffin. If you are paying for a partner's funeral, their bank may be able to release money from their account to help pay funeral expenses before probate is granted.

Ask for help

A counsellor can really help you during this time. Friends and family might be available for you but there comes a time when you don't want to feel like you are burdening them. This is where someone who is not connected to you might be able to help just to get your thoughts together, understand how you are feeling and assist you through your most difficult times.

You will also need friends and family and don't be afraid to say "no" when you don't want to do something, or "yes" when company, a meal, a lift to an appointment or a hand around the house might be just what you need.

Take your time to grieve but when you are ready ask for help to reestablish your social life, put your finances in place and reclaim your life.

WHAT HAPPENS TO YOUR SOCIAL MEDIA ACCOUNTS WHEN YOU DIE?

Your social media accounts, like any other service such as a bank account, have processes to memorialise an account or allow a loved one to maintain and take care of the account. It's worth considering how you would like your social media accounts managed when you die – and ensure that you provide instructions in your estate planning documents.

NOTIFYING THE DEPARTMENT OF HUMAN SERVICES

It's important that you contact the Department of Human Services when someone dies so they can update their Centrelink, Medicare and Child Support records.

Contact details:

Department of Human Services

PO Box 7800

Canberra BC ACT 2610, or Fax 1300 786 102, or visit a service centre

www.humanservices.gov.au/sites/default/files/documents/who-to-notify-checklist.pdf

 QUICK STEPS

- Create a Will. It's ideal to have a solicitor do this for you.
- If you have a Will already, pull it out and review it to make sure it's up to date. If not, see a solicitor to refresh it. Review every three years.
- Create or check your Enduring Power of Attorney.
- Check your super beneficiary nomination – make sure it's current, and that you have eligible beneficiaries named.
- If you own a life insurance policy, check your beneficiary for this too.
- Create a checklist of all your accounts along with pins and passwords. You may want to include social media accounts here too.
- Make sure you have all your documents in one place – and let your loved ones know where to find them. One safe option is with your solicitor.
- Finally, talk to your loved ones about your wishes. It's one of the best ways to ensure that things go to plan.

12

WHAT DOES RETIREMENT LOOK LIKE?

WHAT IS THE FUTURE
LOOKING LIKE WHEN YOU
NO LONGER HAVE TO
SPEND MOST OF YOUR LIFE
WORKING?

🔘 I WANT TO BREAK FREE

Will $1 million be enough to stop working forever?

That's probably the most commonly asked question about retirement. And it is impossible to fully answer. That's because most retirement planning approaches it from the wrong angle. They start with the question of "how much is enough" without first asking a set of far more relevant questions.

Instead we think you should start with you – and your ideal life. It's also a lot more fun and inspiring than defining your world with a number.

After all, this is a major turning point in your life – and probably one that you've been looking forward to for a while. You should be excited by what you're moving towards for this next phase of life – rather than being focused on what you're moving away from.

So, it's time to start thinking about your plans – beyond money.

- What are your dreams for life after work?
- What type of lifestyle would you love to design?
- What do you most want to achieve to create a fulfilling post-work life?

WHEN SHOULD YOU START PLANNING?

There is a saying that you should start planning for your retirement when you receive your first pay check. We certainly didn't do that! Our first pay checks were spent on music, clothes and going out with friends. And we're not alone on this.

Most people are poor at planning for the future. In fact, research[1] suggests the human brain has a weird glitch where it sees our future self as a completely different person – and so the brain acts as if your future self is someone you don't know very well and don't care much about.

---

[1] Hal Hershfield, UCLA Anderson: http://newsroom.ucla.edu/stories/the-stranger-within-connecting-with-our-future-selves

We still believe it's ideal to start planning well in advance – and realistically, to start thinking seriously about what you would like your life to look like about 10 years ahead.

If you have a spouse or partner, it's time to talk

If you're flying solo, you can move straight to designing your ideal life. If you're in a partnership, then it's time to talk and discuss your plans so that together you design your lives to have the best chance of achieving what you each want individually and in tandem.

Just imagine you're dreaming of travelling to all those places on your bucket list, but your partner really wants to keep working for a few more years. Or you want to renovate your home, but your other half wants to buy their dream car. Maybe you want to set money aside for the grandchildren's education and your spouse wants to ensure you have a substantial buffer in your own savings.

It's not that any of these decisions are right or wrong. The mistake is not to communicate well before you plan to retire. If you don't know what your partner is most looking forward to, your differing dreams could make your retirement a nightmare.

DREAM AND DESIGN YOUR NEXT STAGE OF LIFE

Let's dive into our process for planning for when you stop work. The key is to dream and design what you would most love to do in this next phase of your life.

Here are some key questions to consider.

1. When do you want to stop working?

Some people cannot wait to hang up their boots, while others enjoy what they do so much that they want to continue for as long as they can. If you're a couple, it's not unusual for one partner to want to finish work sooner than the other. We often see gaps of around two to three years, where one spouse wants to continue working while the other is ready to find freedom.

2. Do you want to dive in – or will you glide?

Many people want a clear divide between work and play. Others prefer to gradually transition from full-time work to full-time play.

3. What do you want to do with your time?

If you've been used to the structure of work, without a plan to fill your days, stopping employed work can be challenging.

What will you do to enjoy your time and feel fulfilled? Maybe you'll spend time travelling, volunteering, pursuing hobbies, minding grandchildren, spending extra time with family and friend, improving your fitness. If new hobbies or travel are not your thing, maybe consider mentoring or getting involved with new business start ups.

Beyond the day-to-day, identify the things that are on your bucket list. What are the big ticket items that you want to achieve?

Make a list of your top three priorities. If you have a partner, ask them to do the same. Write a letter to your future self to remind you of the things you want to achieve. Be purposeful so you fulfil and don't forget your dreams.

4. Where do you want to live?

Do you want to stay put when you retire or move to new house, a new area or a new region? Some people move to free up capital to live on – whether it's to a smaller house or a regional location. Some move to enjoy a more relaxed lifestyle, or a change of climate. Some shift to be closer to family – particularly once grandchildren arrive on the scene.

Make sure you consider proximity to family and friends, transport and services – and factor it into your plans.

5. How much will it cost?

Now we move into the financial elements of your decision making. Now that you've identified your ideal plans, it's time to work out what you will need to spend to achieve them.

Start with your day-to-day cashflow. Think about how your current costs will change when you are no longer heading to work every day. Then add in the costs for the new activities you'd like to do. Make sure you also consider the bigger ticket items you want to plan for like travel, renovations, the occasional new car and those special things on your bucket list.

To help you do this, head back to our chapter on cashflow – this is as important for your retirement planning as it is throughout your life. It is also helpful to use the Association of Superannuation Funds of Australia (ASFA) retirement benchmarks as a guide. We first introduced these in our Superannuation section. They are tried and tested – based on more than a decade of research.

Known as the Retirement Standard, the data (September quarter 2019) suggests that a couple aged around 65 who own their home and enjoy a comfortable lifestyle are likely to spend around $62,000 a year while a single person needs around $44,000. For a modest lifestyle, a couple needs around $40,000 a year and a single person around $28,000. In terms of what this looks like in the savings you've accumulated by retirement, ASFA estimates that a couple seeking a comfortable lifestyle would need $640,000, and a single person $545,000. It suggests that someone seeking a modest lifestyle – regardless of whether they're a single or couple – may need only $70,000 as their nest egg. This is because they are likely to receive a full Age Pension.

Either way, these numbers assume that individuals own their own home outright and are in fairly healthy shape.

What is considered a modest and comfortable retirement lifestyle?

When we think about a modest lifestyle, we think about our grandparents. They were careful with spending on the most everyday items – after all, they'd lived through World War II and many years of rationing for things we take for granted like clothing, tea, sugar, butter and petrol.

These days, according to ASFA, a modest retirement lifestyle is one where you can afford essential living expenses. You would be able to have some holidays within Australia, and while you can upgrade cars, appliances and electronic items, it would be an occasional and careful purchase.

Now, most of us are probably thinking we'd like a few more creature comforts. Most people we interviewed said that one of the things that was important to them was to live comfortably without having to count every cent, without having to worry about money.

A comfortable lifestyle is one where you can enjoy some of life's little luxuries like occasional international travel and dining out every week. The ASFA Retirement Standard for a comfortable lifestyle includes participating in sports or hobbies, being able to afford private health insurance, and buying things like new white goods, a nice car from time to time, electronics, and good clothes.

Of course, what you think is a comfortable lifestyle could be very different to ours, or to your friends or colleagues. And so the amount you'll need could be more (or less) than the ASFA retirement benchmarks.

We believe that the best thing you can do is to use the ASFA data as a guide – and then build your own picture of your retirement expenses based on how you want to spend your time. We have found that the day-to-day living expenses in the ASFA Standard are pretty consistent regardless of the level of luxury you'd like in the rest of your world. The big ticket items – like theatre subscriptions or club memberships, cars and travel – are often where you'll have differences.

How can I calculate my post-work expenses?

You can use the ASIC Money Smart Budget Planner that we've shared with you as part of our SASSY framework.

www.moneysmart.gov.au/tools-and-resources/calculators-and-apps/
budget-planner

Or if you want a planner that enables you to auto-populate the ASFA Retirement Standard numbers as a guide, this one is very helpful:

www.hesta.com.au/members/forms-resources/calculators/
retirementincomebudget/retirement-income.html

If you find that your annual expenses deliver a much bigger lump sum than you have or are likely to have, by the time you're planning to stop work, then you might need to scale back some of your expenses.

6. How much money will I need as a lump sum?

It is essential to know how much you're likely to need as a lump sum to meet your annual expenses – and to know how you're tracking – so you can plan for a comfortable retirement.

Working out how much money you will need in retirement is not a simple calculation, as things like your investment returns, your drawdown patterns and how long you'll live need more than a calculator – they need a crystal ball.

A useful guide is again provided by ASFA's Retirement Standard. ASFA suggests that for a "comfortable" retirement, single people will need $545,000 in retirement savings, and couples will need $640,000.

Now, of course, if you have additional expenses each year more than ASFA estimates, you'll need a bigger amount. And, if you expect that you'll live longer than most your age, then that will bump up your lump sum requirements too.

Which is why it's important to think about your back up plan – and how you will manage any income or asset shortfall.

7. What's your backup plan?

Life is full of surprises, not all of them happy ones.

Dianne had one of these when her 30-something son had a serious accident, couldn't work for six months and needed ongoing medical care and therapy. He had no private health insurance or income protection, and so she needed to pay the bills.

Sandra found herself caring for her nephew when his parents died in a car accident. She and her husband had sold their business and were planning to travel the world. Fortunately, there were some funds from her sister's estate, but it was going to be a stretch.

9 FORGOTTEN EXPENSES

1. Leisure and hobbies
Now that you have some time on your hands, you'll probably be keen to spend lots of time on all those things you've been putting off doing. Yoga, fitness, learning a language, completing a degree, singing lessons – most activities come with a cost. Make sure you include an allowance for the things that you want to spend time doing.

2. Social connections
Strong positive connections with others is a boost for your mental and physical wellbeing – with less risk of anxiety and depression, higher self-worth, stronger immune system, better recovery from disease, and maybe even a longer life.

3. Healthy lifestyle choices
Ideally you're thinking about choices that enhance your health and prevent disease. They may add to your expenses – whether it's organic produce, a gym membership or personal trainer. You may be able to offset some of this positive spending with a decrease in your not-so-positive spending (like alcohol or take-away). The main thing is to count it in your cashflow.

4. Medical and healthcare
You never know when illness might strike, so it's critical to ensure you have money set aside to care for your healthcare and medical expenses. One of the biggest factors in the increase in retirees' living costs (along with rising costs of power, food and rates) is healthcare.

5. Helping family
It's not just your own health that you need to worry about. If you have elderly parents or adult kids who may be partly dependent on you, you may need to tap into your own savings to provide support.

6. Home expenses
Did you know that the cost of keeping your house maintained and up-to-date is around 1% of its value each year. So for a $1million house, that's

$10,000 a year. Now, while you may not spend that amount every year, if you set aside the funds when you do need to, you'll have the money to spend – without worry.

7. Equipment and appliance fixes and replacement

You know that sinking feeling when you step into the shower and the water's stone cold. The water heater has blown up overnight. Or you're driving along the highway and the car starts making a strange noise. Whether you need to fix or replace, it's going to cost. So it's worth having an allowance in your planned expenditure for when things go bump.

If you are on a low income, you may be eligible for the No Interest Loan Scheme (NILS) – which provides affordable loans of to $1,500 for essential goods and services such as fridges, washing machines and event medical procedures. For more information, go to: https://nils.com.au/

8. Bond for retirement care

We recommend having a plan for how you will pay a bond if you (or your spouse) have to suddenly move into retirement care. If you're single, this is probably top of mind, and you may be thinking you'll sell your home to free up money for a bond. If you're part of a couple, and one of you needs care, you may want to have a separate nest egg so that the other spouse can continue to live in the family home.

9. Longevity

We need to plan for a longer, hopefully healthy, life. "The arc of life has lengthened," said Andrew Scott, co-author with Linda Grattan of *The 100-Year Life: Living and Working in an Age of Longevity*. "We're fitter and healthier for longer. How long are you going to live? You have to think in terms of the future." The first step is to estimate how long you might live – rather than relying on standard life expectancy tables which can't take into account your personal situation. One valuable tool is the SHAPE longevity calculator. It asks you a range of questions on five major areas – Surroundings, Health, Attitude, Parents and Eating – which is why it's called SHAPE. And it will provide an estimate of how long you're likely to live – and need an income to do so in the style to which you have become accustomed!

WHAT DO YOU DO WHEN WHAT YOU HAVE TURNS OUT TO BE NOT ENOUGH?

Reducing your expenses – before and in retirement – is an option. So do go back and re-read our section on cashflow, in Chapter 2 Be Sassy.

The other option is to increase your income. Here we share just five interesting ideas.

1. Delay your retirement: Every additional year you work is another year of earnings that can add to savings, and one less year of living that is paid for out of savings. Additionally, if you become eligible for a Centrelink pension, delaying your retirement date could mean you boost your age pension income.

2. Transition into retirement: Maybe you can work part time or casually. Perhaps you can start an encore career. We know women who are using their experience and wisdom well by mentoring, joining advisory boards, consulting and teaching. Others have become retail assistants, medical centre receptionists, tutors and legal consultants. Even a little extra income can make a difference. And if you find something new that you love, it could easily beat 30 years of free time. The key is being able to work on your own terms – with less stress, flexible hours.

3. Turn lifestyle assets into cash: Do you have things in your life that you don't use? Or maybe you use them occasionally and no longer need to own. This might be a second car that could be replaced by ride share or public transport. Or valuables that you no longer value like jewellery from an ex, art work that you can take or leave? Even clothing or household items that you could sell on a second-hand marketplace?

4. Earn passive income: The wonders of technology have opened up all sorts of ways for individuals to earn extra income without working in the traditional sense. Here's a few ideas:
   - Rent your home or a room: If you're going away on holidays, you could make your home available for rent on a site like Airbnb. If you have a home with a spare room or two, you could rent those.

- Dog walk: If you enjoy a good walk, why not take along a furry friend or two. There are many companies that connect dog owners with walkers, as well as opportunities through sites like Airtasker.
- Pet-sit: many owners seeing their pets as members of the family rather than as merely companions. This means that pet owners are spending significant sums on the care of their pets. So, if you're an animal lover, this could be your chance to pet-sit, provide doggy day care, dog board, and even house sit while earning a tidy sum.
- Take paid surveys: Both locally and internationally, you can access very good paid online survey sites – some offer vouchers, others offer cash just for sharing your opinions.
- Chat in English: There is a demand for people to talk in English to help students learning English in a formal educational context to gain real life practice.

WILL YOU STILL BE REPAYING YOUR MORTGAGE AT 70?

Nearly half of all homeowners aged 55 to 64 are still paying off a mortgage, up from just 14 per cent 30 years ago, according to new research. The study by the Australian Housing and Urban Research Institute (AHURI) suggested that the runaway property market was exacerbating the issue, as price growth ran away from wage growth. The issue is not only the rapid rise in the proportion of near-retiree home owners carrying a mortgage, but the increased amount of debt relative to income.

In a low interest rate environment, maintaining a mortgage may make perfect sense.

However, should interest rates rise, some people may need to work past their ideal retirement age not as a lifestyle choice, but a financial necessity.

Either way, it's vital to consider your options – and ensure that repaying your mortgage before or after retirement is in your plan.

5. Downsize your home: for many Australians, their home is their most valuable asset. It may be an option to convert part of that value from a non-income earning asset by downsizing. (You could also consider other options like a reverse mortgage. These come with limits and costs, so need to be handled with care.)

Each individual idea could boost your retirement savings enough to solve your gap. However, weave them together, and you have a magical bag of tricks to substantially improve your financial position.

BENEFITS IN RETIREMENT

Depending on your financial situation, you may be able to access certain government benefits.

If you are eligible for the Age Pension, you may also be able to access other benefits including Pensioner Concession Card and rent assistance.

If you're not eligible for the Age Pension you may still be able to get the Seniors Health Card to access certain discounts.

The eligibility rules and thresholds change regularly, so we recommend contacting Centrelink or attending one of the government's free financial education seminars for retirees who want to understand more about the Age Pension and other benefits.

It's your retirement: do what brings you joy

You've worked hard to get to this exciting new stage. Remember, that while your life should always be about you and your values, goals and priorities – at retirement this is even more important. This is a time when the shoulds shouldn't matter. It's a time when you don't need to keep up with any Joneses. Instead, it's a time for you to do the things that bring you joy.

Maybe you're focused on enjoying life's essential pleasures, like minding your grandchildren and walks with your dog along the beach. Or maybe you're going to swing for the fences and climb Kilimanjaro. Scale should not matter. Be conscious, plan well, and make sure your retirement life is what you've dreamed and designed.

TAKIN' CARE OF BUSINESS

Super smarts when starting or finishing in a job

Like any big change in circumstances, changing jobs is a good time to take stock of your finances. Yet in the mayhem, many people fail to take care of their super. Don't make this common mistake.

Starting a new role

Most employees are entitled to receive superannuation. When you start a new role, you can choose where your super money goes: into a fund you already have, your new employer's default fund or a completely new one that you like.

Sometimes an employer fund has a better deal on fees, and perhaps may include other benefits such as subsidised insurance.

However, don't just default into the employer fund without doing your homework. Dive into the detail and compare benefits and fees – or you could end up paying more money than you need to.

Consolidating super – that is, putting it in one place with one super fund – can be a good idea, not only to save fees, but also to help you keep track of your money. However, there may be a downside: you could have insurance cover in your current funds that you could lose if you merge them.

It can be confusing, so do ask for professional help – see a financial adviser who can help you compare and translate some of the rules and jargon that come with superannuation.

Leaving a job

There are various ways you might be leaving a role: you may be moving to another role, your role may be redundant or you may be looking to stop working altogether.

Here are three important super considerations:

1 If you have an employer super plan, your fees may increase once you are no longer employed at the company.

2 If you have insurance (life and TPD) through your super check what happens when you finish work? Does your insurance cover continue, or does it end? If you wish to keep it, can you elect to continue it personally? If your employer has been paying for your insurance, what will the new premium cost be? If your insurances stop and you want to reinstate them down the track you may have to be assessed again and as you age you may find you have had incidents or conditions which may affect your premiums. So if you think you would like to keep your insurance cover where it is, you need to check what to do with your super fund before you end your employment.

3 If you are leaving a job and don't have another role lined up, you will need to check the rules on your income protection insurance. It will lapse after a certain period and to keep it up you will need to work a minimum number of hours per week (usually around 24).

REDUNDANCY

You are favourably taxed when leaving a job – and it is based on full years in the role. If you are very close to your work anniversary when you receive a redundancy you may like to check with your employer if there is a way to meet it – either by extending your role, or giving you leave without pay, or perhaps putting you in a different role for a short period.

Insurance tip

Often if you're finishing a role, or even thinking about finishing, you get organised and arrange things like health checks. But wait! Before doing your medical checks, it's a good idea to do your insurance review. That's because when you apply for or review insurance cover, the insurer usually has specific medical tests they need you to do – and they cover the cost. So doing this first is likely to be more efficient and free.

Mentally fit

When things are not going well at work, before you leave you may be tempted to take stress leave. Please be aware that this can sometimes affect your premiums and conditions when wanting to obtain a new insurance policy.

 QUICK STEPS

- Spend time to plan your priorities for your ideal life. If you have a partner, make sure you discuss and determine your joint plans.
- Work out what type of lifestyle you'd like in retirement – the short cut way to do this is to look at the ASFA modest and comfortable lifestyles and use them as a guide.
- Based on your lifestyle choices, consider how much money you're likely to need – you can use the ASFA estimates of the lump sum amount for different lifestyles and then adjust up or down from there.
- Calculate how much you're likely to have – you'll need to have an idea of how much you have now, how much you're likely to save and your likely investment return. Use a retirement calculator to help you.
- Do you have a gap? Think about how you'll look to close it – check out our tips on closing the gap, and on earning a little extra income.
- Find out what you may be entitled to from the Government. You might be surprised.

13

SEEKING FINANCIAL ADVICE

SEEKING PROFESSIONAL ADVICE MAY BE EXPENSIVE BUT MAKING MISTAKES ON YOUR OWN MAY BE MORE COSTLY IN THE LONG RUN

 HELP IS ON ITS WAY

You can access help with your personal finances easily. There are many online resources – like savings calculators and budget tools – and numerous investment and super funds that you can access to help you manage your money. Yet, most successful investors engage a financial adviser.

A WHOLE NEW WORLD

Why seek the help of an adviser?

It's like exercising. You can probably do it yourself, but engaging a professional trainer keeps you disciplined and on track and, perhaps more importantly, they'll push you to do tougher moves like planks and squats, which build stronger, more sturdy muscles to sustain your health over your lifetime.

Often people seek out a financial adviser when their money matters have become too complicated for them to manage themselves. Or, they're facing a significant financial and life change or challenge. Sometimes it's just a gnawing sense of discomfort that won't go away.

Financial advisers know the ins, outs, and strategies that can help you make the most of your money and avoid money mistakes. One of the biggest benefits of having a professional financial adviser is to take the stress out of navigating complex life and financial decisions.

Yet, this is only part of the picture. Kate says: "Clients come for better financial outcomes, and stay for better sleep at night".

"You have a full sensory experience when you go to see and hear a live performance. Without a financial planner it's like being home with the stereo on."

When should you see a financial adviser?

Earlier than you think. One of the most common refrains is: "I wish I'd done this sooner." Here are some triggers when seeing a financial adviser could help you financially – and to sleep better at night.

1. Personal life changes

- Moving in together, becoming engaged, or getting married. Starting on the same page with your significant other is important as different money values and saving behaviours can destroy a relationship.
- Having a baby. This is about more than adjusting to a period of parental leave, less income and more expenses. It's about establishing a new life plan: what will your work patterns and caring patterns be as parents; how will childcare fit into the picture – and what type do you want and can you afford; how do you direct your incomes into spending and savings buckets; what benefits might you be entitled to; when is it time to start planning for school, what type of schooling do you want and can you afford? And of course, have you established or updated your Wills and estate planning documents?
- Changing career or redundancy. Chances are you will have career shifts, sabbaticals and re-training in your working life. This could be no earned income for a year. How do you set up your assets to pay you a regular income when you're not earning? How do you make sure you've got enough money to take time out without worrying about money?
- Separating or divorcing. Yes, there'll be an asset split. That's the tip of the iceberg. There's so much more to consider: what really is your overall financial position; what's the most cost- and tax-effective way to share the asset pool; how do you provide for children if you have them; how do you protect assets from future partners for the eventual benefit of your children; what concessions might be available to you. It's a highly emotive time (Kate knows, she's been through it) and you need an adviser to give you objective advice to help you through.
- Retirement – when you finally hang up your boots and are no longer earning an income from employment.
- When disaster strikes – like becoming seriously ill or injured, or the death of your partner, child or someone you love.

2. Wealth changes
- New job. You've got a new role or promotion. Maybe it brings a significant pay increase. Perhaps a vested bonus structure, equity stake or additional employee benefits. How do you make the most of it without seeing it eaten away in tax?
- New house – which usually comes with new liabilities!
- Inheritance – which can create pleasure and also strain. How do you best use the money? How do you ensure you protect it?

3. Emotional guidance
- Calm amidst the share market storm. Share markets are often volatile – and most people value objective advice and support. William Bernstein, author of the Investors Manifesto has said: "At the end of the day, how well you do over the course of your investment life is mostly dependent upon that 2 per cent of the time in the markets when it looks like the world is ending... That's where the value of a human being comes in."
- Clarity and consciousness. A good financial adviser can push you to be more honest about your finances. Most people don't have a clear view of their annual expenses – and don't want to! Yet once they do, they feel a sense of empowerment. As you know from our earlier section on cashflow, we believe you need to be conscious of where e ach dollar goes. This is the foundation of a lifetime financial plan – and can make all the difference in achieving your goals.

HOW CAN YOU FIND A GOOD FINANCIAL ADVISER?

The best way is usually a referral from someone you trust. Ask for a recommendation from people you know who are most like you. Make sure they've been working with their adviser for a number of years – as this gives you the best chance of seeing what impact their adviser has made.

You could also use a "find an adviser" service through an industry association to locate an adviser in your area. To get you started, here are services from the main financial advice professional bodies in Australia:

- Association of Financial Advisers' Find an adviser service: *www.afa.asn.au/find-afa-financial-adviser*
- Financial Planning Association's Find a planner service: *https://fpa.com.au/*

Another helpful source, called the Most Trusted Advisers, is provided by an independent group called the Beddoes Institute. This includes advisers who have been evaluated based on a comprehensive survey of their clients, and then selected as the most trusted by the Beddoes Institute: *www.mosttrustedadvisers.com/*

What questions should you ask?

The first step in selecting an adviser is to assess what we call the "above the line" elements. These are "table stakes" for being a good adviser.

You can do this homework online – using industry association listings and adviser websites. This could save you a lot of headache later.

Questions to shortlist advisers that may suit you are:

- **What are the adviser's qualifications and credentials?**
  They should have sound technical qualifications including a degree and specialist financial planning designation. Advisers are also required to be a member of a professional body and sign up to a Code of Ethics.
- **How are they licensed?**
  A financial adviser must be employed or authorised by an Australian Financial Services Licence. Check the ASIC Money Smart financial advisers register – see box on p218.
- **What is the adviser's experience?**
  This includes experience in financial advice and in working with clients like you.
- **How is the adviser remunerated?**
  Do they charge a fee for service and if so, how is this calculated? You want to understand how they earn every single dollar that they get paid. Look for their Financial Services Guide on their website (these can sometimes be tricky to find!).

- **What are their typical product costs?**
  The costs associated with investing – whether it's super or personal investments – are usually not something clients find out until they have selected an adviser and received a formal plan. However, it's better to know your costs of implementing the advice recommendations before you become a client. And remember, a good rule of thumb is that your total cost of investing should be no more than 1% p.a. of the value of the assets being invested.

- **What financial planning services do they offer?**
  Your ideal adviser is one whose expertise lies in the areas in which you need the most help.

- **What products and services do they recommend?**
  Are they aligned with any particular product provider? Or do you prefer an adviser who operates separately?

Once you have your shortlist of advisers it's time to ask the "below the line" questions – these are the things that might not be so visible and go deeper into their values and approach.

- **What is your firm's philosophy?**
  You're looking for an adviser who focuses on you, who is interested in your goals, aspirations, risks, and fears – not themselves. This means that you want to steer clear of an adviser that tells you all about their stellar stock market performance or their ability to pick stocks or time markets (as we've shared in the Investing section, the reality is that it is almost impossible for anyone to consistently beat the market). The value of a great adviser is not to beat the market, but to be your personal finance officer.

- **What is your approach to investing?**
  While there is no right answer, you want your adviser to have is a well-thought-out, evidence-based process. Listen for cues like: achieving the best returns the market has to offer; low cost investing; starting with your risk tolerance; understanding the returns you need to accomplish your goals.

HOW WAS THAT AWARD ACHIEVED?

Be careful of shiny awards. While some financial advisers promote awards, it's important to realise that many very fine financial advisers simply don't wish to tout their accomplishments and so don't seek out industry awards. It's also important to check the criteria for any adviser awards to see how they are earned. Some awards are popularity contests based on voting by peers, some are earned by achieving revenue or sales targets, while the most valuable are based on a rigorous business evaluation and tough judging.

- **How will you work with my other professionals?**
  While your accountant and lawyer have particular jobs they will do for you, a good adviser will overlap in areas like tax planning, self managed super fund management and estate planning. Ideally you want to work with someone who is happy to work with your existing team or can introduce you to trusted professionals in their network to get integrated, not conflicting or confusing, advice.

- **Based on what you know about me, why do you think I am a suitable client?**
  You don't want to work with an adviser who takes everyone who walks in their door. Their answer should show that they have a good understanding of your situation, your objectives and concerns and how they can add value.

- **Can you tell me about a time when you helped a client like me?**
  This is a good clue to their ability to add value for you. You want to know that they have expertise and experience helping clients with similar circumstances or challenges.

- **How will we know I'm making progress?**
  You want to know if you're making the right sort of progress financially. This is less about investment performance and more about your progress towards your personal goals. Are you improving your overall financial position? Are you achieving the things that you set out to achieve that take money and planning to achieve?

- **How will we communicate?**
  How often can you expect to meet or have other types of contact. What happens if you have a question? A great adviser will seek to build a partnership with you – and so you need to understand how your communications might work both ways.

  Remember, you want to select someone you trust, and with whom you can create a strong and open relationship – to give you the very best chance of achieving your financial goals.

How do you get the most out of your relationship with your adviser?

1. Ask questions. If you want to clarify what's recommended and why. If you don't understand. If you're worried or concerned – about anything.

2. Participate. The best advice relationships are a two-way street. So, make sure you participate in decision making and collaborate with your adviser to ensure that you get the very best strategy and outcome for your needs.

3. Inform. Make sure you provide full and accurate information to your adviser. And update your adviser of any significant changes in your world. Let them know before you make any big changes or decisions. Most times, an adviser can help you navigate the financial aspects of your change or decision – there just might be some clever strategies you can use in the planning stage that you don't want to miss out on.

4. Engage. Keep up the discipline of participating in your regular advisory meetings. Even if you don't think you have anything important to discuss, the regular rhythm of meetings is an important reminder of the things that you need to do to stay on track, and of your progress.

5. Respond. Answer emails. Return phone calls. Do your homework on time.

6. Take responsibility. Read the advice you're given. Review minutes. Read the fine print. While you're employing a professional to help you, your financial wellbeing is still your responsibility.

7. Take advice. You've hired a professional because you wanted expert guidance on financial and investment decisions. So, while it's important to have robust discussions with your adviser, you also need to get comfortable trusting your adviser's judgement and avoid trying to second-guess their recommendations. Of course, if you don't feel that you're on the same page, or you feel uncomfortable with the advice, you need to discuss this with your adviser and perhaps consider whether your current choice is the best adviser for you.

8. Enjoy. Your relationship with your adviser should also be fulfilling and fun. Make sure that you enjoy the ride.

CHECK THE FINANCIAL ADVISERS REGISTER

The register enables you to check on an adviser's history, qualifications and current employment status before you approach them about getting advice. It includes such things as if they are a member of a relevant professional body or industry association, whether they have been the subject of disciplinary action by ASIC, how they are licensed.

www.moneysmart.gov.au/investing/financial-advice/
financial-advisers-register

Source: ASIC Money Smart

 QUICK STEPS

- Decide what type of advice you're looking for – do you want help with a particular transaction, or are you seeking a long term relationship?

- Ask for a referral to an adviser from people who have a similar situation and values to you. Or try one of the sites we've provided.

- Do your homework – use our questions to help you find an adviser who you feel you can trust.

- Be involved – after all, it's your money and your life.

BEST PIECES OF FINANCIAL ADVICE I'VE BEEN GIVEN

"YOU CAN'T ALWAYS GET WHAT YOU WANT"

"Look at now, the medium term and the long-term future and allow yourself some enjoyment in all three. In other words, don't save everything for the future."

- Cynthia

"When I was growing up, other families had nice cars, lovely furniture – they remodelled their kitchens and spent money at Xmas. We didn't. Our money went into investment properties, so we lived with older cars, outdated furniture etc. I still live like that, which surprises me. I also have investment properties behind me."

- Alethea

"TO CHANGE YOUR LIFE, YOU NEED TO CHANGE YOUR PRIORITIES."

- NICOLE

"Annual income twenty pounds, annual expenditure nineteen [pounds] nineteen [shillings] and six [pence], result happiness. Annual income twenty pounds, annual expenditure twenty pounds ought and six, result misery."

- Charles Dickens
(requoted by Andy)

"You can't afford poor quality. It costs money. It costs money to fix, it costs money to replace."

- Naomi

"When I was in primary school my father would say: 'Money doesn't grow on trees, you need to work for it and save to get what you want'. That led to a lifetime of good habits."

- Sharon

"SAVE, SAVE, SAVE - AND THEN SAVE SOME MORE."

- SOPHIE

When I was growing up I worked in our family business... having saved a reasonable sum my mum suggested "why don't you buy the bank rather than putting your money in it?" That led to my first share purchase in ANZ at age 13. I loved the quarterly dividends that magically turned up for no effort on my part.

- Julia

"WALK AWAY BEFORE YOU MAKE A PURCHASE. IF YOU CAN DO WITHOUT IT, KEEP WALKING."

- LISA

"A credit card is for payment convenience, not a funding source. Only use your credit card what you are able to repay in full when it's due."

- David

"Don't ever buy a depreciating asset such as a car on credit and, still on cars, if you can't afford to lose or repair it, you can't really afford it."

- Louise

"Have three to six months of rent or mortgage repayments saved. If you don't have that, start putting it together now. Every bit makes a difference. Saving and seeing that balance grow gives an incredible sense of security and safety that stands the test of time. The excitement of buying that new shiny thing never lasts as long."

- Sally

"Never become financially reliant on a man. Control your life yourself (from my dad...I reckon for a 70s dad he was way ahead of his time)."

- Susan

"If you wouldn't buy it full price, don't buy it on sale." Many people focus on saving money when they buy things. You'll save far more money by focusing on not buying things you don't truly need.

- Kate

ACKNOWLEDGEMENTS

"I thank my brains trust for their faith, unwavering support and for being so damn smart, generous and inspiring always. I wish every woman could have such a group surrounding her for good times, tough times, and all the times in between.

I thank my parents who managed to ingrain in me some good financial habits, despite myself, and whose voices I still hear when I am buying big and saving little.

And I thank my partner Glenn who has never doubted me."

Julia

"I want to thank my husband Tony for his hare-brained humour, and constant kindness as I fit writing this book in the crazy fabric of our life.

To my sons Ben and Connor, for your sparky fresh thinking each week at breakfast, and for shining your bright light in the world.

To my amazing women friends who shared their stories, and offered formidable and unfettered feedback on my ideas.

To my parents for creating a space where I learnt to be responsible with money – though I don't think I appreciated it at the time! And to my grandparents for their hard-learned wisdom about how to do more with less."

Kate

From us both, we thank the myriad of finance and investment experts we've read, listened to and whose ideas have been now seamlessly integrated into our mode and method. We stand on the shoulders of giants.

To the many women we interviewed, thank you for giving us an insight into your world, sharing your vices and vulnerabilities around money, and being as excited as we were about creating a book on the joy of money.

And to you, our readers, we wish you success born of knowledge, and trust this book really does help you discover the joy of money.

Kate and Julia